D0913450

Few books published by Corgi
have aroused so much interest
and correspondence as have
Lobsang Rampa's bestsellers,
the titles of which appear
overleaf.

Each one is immensely readable
and thought-provoking in its
exploration of the realms of the
Occult and the Astral.

Also by T. Lobsang Rampa

and published by Corgi Books

T. Lobsang Rampa

Wisdom of the
Ancients

CORGI BOOKS
A DIVISION OF TRANSWORLD PUBLISHERS LTD

WISDOM OF THE ANCIENTS
A CORGI BOOK 0 552 11532 0

First publication in Great Britain

PUBLISHING HISTORY
Corgi edition published 1965
Corgi edition reprinted 1966
Corgi edition reprinted 1968
Corgi edition reprinted 1969
Corgi edition reprinted 1970
Corgi edition reprinted 1971
Corgi edition reprinted 1972
Corgi edition reprinted 1974
Corgi edition reprinted 1975
Corgi edition reprinted 1977
Corgi edition reissued 1980
Corgi edition reprinted 1981

This book is set in 10 pt Granjon

Corgi Books are published by Transworld Publishers Ltd.,
Century House, 61–63 Uxbridge Road,
Ealing, London W5 5SA.
Made and printed in Great Britain by
Hunt Barnard Printing Ltd., Aylesbury, Bucks.

To
The Lady Ku'ei
who taught me
many
Siamese Cat
words
and always encouraged me!

CONTENTS

WHAT THIS BOOK IS

SUCH a lot of people like to have big words. Such a lot of people mess up the whole thing when they go in for Big Words.

I like small words. It is so much easier to say what one means with small words. After all, if we are going to read a book in English, or Spanish, we do not normally need Sanskrit or Hindustani or Chinese words. However, some people like Big Words.

This is an honest attempt to give you a Dictionary of certain words, and to go into some detail about the meanings. In some instances the meaning could well constitute a monograph.

Monograph? MONOGRAPH? What is a monograph? A short essay on one subject will explain it.

But let us get on with our little Dictionary because that is what you will be interested in. I thought that first of all I should say—Just A Word!

WE will start with the letter A. I cannot think of any which comes before, so the first word is:

ABHINIVESHA: This indicates possessiveness restricted to a love of life on Earth. It is an attachment to the things of life and a fear of death because of the loss of possessions which that will bring. Misers love their money, and they fear death because death will part them from their money. To those who suffer from this particular complaint I will say that no one has yet succeeded in taking even a penny into the next life!

ABSTINENCES: We have to abstain, or refrain from doing, certain things if we are to progress on the road to spirituality. We must refrain or abstain from injuring others; we must refrain from telling lies. Theft—we must avoid theft because it is altering the material balance of another person if we steal from them. Sensuality? That is an impure form of sex, and while pure sex can elevate one, sensuality can ruin one spiritually as well as financially!

Greed is a thing of which we should not be guilty. Mankind is lent money or abilities in order that we may help others. If we are greedy and refuse to help in case of genuine need, then we may be sure that help will be refused us in time of need.

If one can honour the Five Abstinences—abstention from injuring others, abstention from lies, abstention from theft, abstention from sensuality, and abstention from greed, then one can be at peace with the world, although it does not follow that the world can be at peace with one.

ACHAMANA: This is a rite practised by those of the Hindu belief. It is a rite in which a worshipper purifies himself by thinking of pure things while sipping water and sprinkling water around him. In some ways it is similar to the sprinkling of water during a Christian ceremony. The Hindu, having done this, can then retire into a peaceful state of meditation.

ACHARYA: This is a word for a spiritual teacher, or, if you prefer it, a Guru. Acharya is frequently a suffix to the name of some revered religious teacher.

ADHARMA: This indicates lack of virtue, lack of righteousness. The poor fellow probably does not abstain from any of the Five Abstinences.

AGAMA: A Scripture, or in Tibet a Tantra. It can be used to indicate any work which trains one in mystical or metaphysical worship.

AGAMI KARMA: This is the correct term for Karma. It means that the physical and mental acts performed by one in the body affect one's future incarnations. In the Christian Bible there is a statement that as one sows so shall one reap, which is much the same as saying that if you sow the seeds of wickedness then you shall reap wickedness, but if you sow the seeds of good and help for others then the same shall be returned to you 'a thousandfold.' Such is Karma.

AHAMKARA: The mind is divided into various parts, and Ahamkara is the sort of traffic director which receives sense impressions and establishes them as the form of facts which we know, and which we can call to mind at will.

AHIMSA: This was the policy followed by Gandhi, a policy of peace, of non-violence. It is refraining from harming any other creature in thought, deed, or word. It is, in fact, another way of saying, 'Do as you would be done by.'

AI: The shortest known way of saying equal love for all without discrimination as to race, creed, colour, or form. When we are capable of truly fulfilling the meaning of the word Ai, then we do not have to stay on this world any longer, because we are too pure to stay here any longer.

AJAPA: This is a special Mantra. The Easterner believes that breath goes out with the sound of 'AJ,' and is taken in with the sound 'SA.' Hansa is the sound of human breathing. 'HA,' breath going out; 'N' as a conjunction; 'SA,' breath coming in. We make that subconscious sound fifteen times in one minute, or twenty-one thousand six hundred times in twenty-four hours. Animals also have their own particular rate; a cat does it twenty-four times a minute, a tortoise three times a minute.

Some people consider that the Ajapa Mantra is also an unconscious, or rather, a sub-conscious prayer, which means 'I am That.'

AJNACHAKRA: This is the sixth of the commonly accepted figure of seven of the known Yogic centres of consciousness. Actually there are nine such centres, but that would be delving too deeply into Tibetan lore to explain here.

Ajnachakra is the Lotus at the eyebrow level, a Lotus, in this case, with only two petals. This is a part of the sixth-sense mechanism. It leads to clairvoyance, internal vision, and knowledge of the world beyond this world.

AKASHA: Many people refer to this as ether, but a rather better definition would be—that which fills all space between worlds, molecules, and everything. The matter from which everything else is formed.

It should be remembered that this matter is common throughout our own planetary system, but it does not at all follow that other universes have the same form of matter. You can say that the human body consists of blood cells, flesh cells, and, yet in a different part, bone cells.

AKASHIC: This is usually used when referring to the Akashic Record.

It is difficult to explain to a three-dimensional world that which is an occurrence in a more multi-dimensional world, but it may be regarded like this:

Imagine that you are a ciné photographer who has always existed and will always exist, and you have an unlimited supply of film (and someone to process it for you!). From the beginning of time you have photographed everything that ever happened anywhere to anyone and everyone. You are still photographing events of the present day. That represents the Akashic Record; everything that has ever happened is impressed upon the ether as are light impulses recorded on ciné film, or a voice record can be impressed upon recording tape.

In addition to this, because of the multi-dimensional world in which it is recorded, there also can be recorded the very strong probabilities which affect everyone on Earth and off the Earth. You can imagine that you are in a city; you are on a street, a car is coming along, it passes you, and it disappears from your sight, you have no knowledge of what is happening to it. But supposing, instead, that you were up in a balloon and you could look down and you could see the road for miles ahead. You could see the car rushing along, and you could see perhaps an obstacle in the road which the car would not be able to avoid. Thus you would see misfortune coming to that driver before he was aware of it. Or you can regard the case of the timetable: Timetables are issued indicating the probability that a train or a bus, a ship or a plane, will leave at a certain time from a certain place, and according to the timetable, which is merely a record of probabilities, will arrive at a certain place at a certain time. In nearly every instance the vehicle does arrive.

When considering the Akashic Record it is worth remembering that if you could travel instantly to a far distant planet and you had a very special instrument, the light which was arriving from the Earth (light has a speed, remember) might show what was happening on Earth a hundred, a thousand, or ten thousand years ago. With your special instrument you would be able to see the Earth as it was a thousand years ago.

The Akashic Record goes beyond that because it shows the strong probability of what is going to happen. The probabilities confronting a nation are very much stronger, are much more certain, than in the case of individuals, and those people who are specially trained can enter the astral state and they can consult the Akashic Record to see what has happened, what is happening in any part of the world, and what are the terrifically strong probabilities for the future. It is a very much, in fact, like going to some news theatre and seeing a film. If you know from the programme what film is on at a certain time you can go and see just that.

ANAHATA CHAKRA: The symbolism of this Chakra is The Wheel or The Lotus. The symbolism of the East refers to it as a stylised Wheel, which is also a stylised Lotus. In Tibet it is The Lotus only.

This is a Chakra at the level of the heart. It has twelve petals of a golden colour. When one can see the aura one can observe that sometimes the gold is tinged with red, at other times it will be streaked or flecked with a dark blue showing the different moods, and the different stages of evolution of the person.

Below this Anahata centre is another manifestation of The Lotus, one with an eight-petal arrangement which stirs and waves slightly when one does meditation. It stirs and waves like the sea anemone which we can see in an aquarium.

When one can see the aura, one can see the rays of light which make it resemble The Flowering Lotus or The Wheel, depending upon one's sense of imagery, the mechanical or horticultural.

The Anahata Chakra is the fourth of the seven commonly known Yogic centres of consciousness. Actually, as already stated previously, there are more than seven.

ANAHATA SHABDA: This means a sound which is not an actually perceived sound. Instead, it is an impression of sound which is often heard during meditation when one has reached a certain stage. The sound, of course, is that of the Mantra Om.

ANANDA: Pure joy. Joy and pleasure unalloyed by material concepts. It indicates the bliss and happiness which one experiences when one can get out of the body consciously and be aware of the absolute rapture of being free, even for a time, from the cold and desolate clay sheath which is the human body on Earth.

ANATMA: The meaning of this is 'This is the World of Illusion.' Upon this world, this Earth, we think that only material things matter. People grub in the dirt for money, and pile up masses of money (some of them!). No one has ever taken a single penny into the next life, but they still rush after the material things which we leave when we depart from this world.

ANGAS: An indication of things which one must obey in order to progress in spiritual rather than physical Yoga. One must progress and correctly observe meditation, breath control, advanced meditation, and contemplation. One must also specifically remember the Golden Rule which means—Do as you would be done by.

ANNAMAYAKOSHA: That big word just means the physical sheath or body which encases the spirit. When one is coming back into the physical body after being consciously in the astral one does not even use such a word as that to express one's feelings of the cold and clammy mess into which one must painfully clamber, one uses a much worse word. But—Annamayakosha is the technical word.

ANTAHKARANA: Eastern philosophy, Vedanta philosophy,

uses this word when referring to the mind as it is used in controlling a physical body.

APANA: Some of the words of the far, far East are remarkably explicit in their meanings. Sanskrit is not bound by the conventions of many Western languages. We cannot always use precisely the same meanings, so let us just put down the meaning of Apana as all that which has to do with excretion, the various orifices, processes, etc.

In the aura appropriately enough it appears as a dark red, or dark-brown red, colour which swirls and twists and then spreads out like a turgid pool.

APARIGRAHA: This is the fifth of the Abstinences. It indicates that one should take the Middle Way in all things, being not too good yet not too bad, avoiding extremes and being balanced.

ARHAT: This is one who has attained to a perfect understanding of that which is beyond life. It indicates that one has discarded the ideas that:

1. The body is important.
2. Uncertainty about the correct Path to take.
3. Dependence upon rigid rules.
4. Likings arising from an imperfect memory of a past life.
5. Dislikings arising from an imperfect memory of a past life.

ASANA: This is a posture, or sitting position, and is used when preparing to meditate.

The Great Masters never laid down fixed rules about how one should sit, they merely stated that one should be comfortable and at ease, but since those times various people who are not by any means Great Masters have tried to create a sensation, tried to increase their own self-advertised status by ordering that their Yogic students should indulge in all sorts of ridiculous and fantastic contortions.

The only thing you have to do in order to meditate is to sit comfortably, and then you are definitely in the correct position. It does not matter if you sit with your legs crossed, or your legs straight out or straight down, so long as you are comfortable that is all that is required in the posture.

ASAT: All those things which are unreal or illusory. This is

14

the World of Illusion, the world of unreality. The World of the Spirit is the real world.

The opposite of Asat is Sat, that is, those things which are real.

ASHRAMA: This means a place wherein Teacher and pupils reside. Often it is used to denote a hermitage, but it can also be used to indicate the four main stages into which life on Earth is divided. Those stages are:

1. The celibate student.

2. A married person who thus is not celibate. The person does not have to be a student.

3. Retirement and contemplation.

4. The monastic life, and monastic, you may like to be reminded, indicates a solitary life.

ASMITA: Conceit, egoism, and the puffed-up pride of the unevolved human. As a person evolves Asmita disappears.

ASTEYA: A name for the third of the Abstinences. The third of the Abstinences exhorts one not to steal, and when one is warned not to steal it means that you must not steal in thought nor in deed, nor must you covet the property of another person.

ASTRAL: This is a term which is generally used to indicate the place or condition that one reaches when one is out of the body. It is a place where one can meet one's friends who have passed over after leaving the body in so-called death, and who are waiting to make plans so that they may reincarnate.

The astral world could be considered as corresponding roughly to the Christian Paradise, a place which is an in-between place, a meeting-place, but not the ultimate Heaven.

ASTRAL TRAVELLING: When a person lays down to rest the physical mechanism of the body becomes quiescent. The physical functions slow down, but the astral form, or Soul, or Ego, or Atman, does not rest in the body but goes out of the body into the astral plane.

One can liken it to this; when one goes to bed one takes off one's day clothes and lays aside the day clothes. In the same way the astral body lays aside the flesh body as we lay aside the clothing of the day.

It is worth noting that there are various planes, or stages, of the astral world. One can do astral travelling and travel from one's country of origin or country of residence to various parts of the physical world; one can go from England to Australia, or Australia to China, or anywhere like that. It depends on what one has to do how one uses one's astral time.

A person who is very evolved and perhaps is living his last life on Earth is busy always in the astral, and the more evolved a person, the farther he travels in the astral.

Astral travelling is easy provided one practises. It needs practice only, or perhaps one should say, practice and patience. All animals can do it, as all animals can do clairvoyance and telepathy.

It should also be mentioned here that the Paradise of the astral world can, in some instances, be purgatory for those who have misbehaved on the Earth! People meet in the astral and plan what they are going to do in the physical. Unfortunately, so many people forget their wondrous intentions and do only that which suits them.

It is recommended that one practises astral travelling because it is the most stupendously wonderful feeling that one can imagine to rise up at the end of one's Silver Cord, and watch the cities of the Earth beneath one's gaze, and then perhaps soar into space and look at other worlds. Or if one deserts the physical world completely one can go into the metaphysical worlds, and see and talk with friends who have gone on before.

ATMA: Some people call it Atman. Vedantic philosophy regards the Atma or Atman as the overriding spirit, the Overself, the Ego, or the Soul.

AURA: Just as a magnet has lines of force about it so has the body lines of force, but these are lines of force in different colours, covering a wider range of colours than human sight could ever see without the aid of clairvoyant abilities.

The auric colours flare out from the most important centres of the body, and unite to form a swirling egg-shaped mass with the blunt end of the egg at the top.

A good aura can extend for perhaps six feet from its possessor.

A trained clairvoyant by seeing the colours of the aura can detect incipient illness or disease. Later there will be instruments for seeing the aura in colour (so that the non-clairvoyant can see it, that is), and by applying a suitable heterodyne signal, defective shades of the aura will be cured of illness.

The aura must not be confused with the etheric, which see under E.

AVASTHAS: A word descriptive of the three states of consciousness which are:

1. The waking state, during which one is in the body more or less conscious of things going on about one.

2. The dream world, in which fantasies of the mind become intermingled with the realities experienced during even partial astral travel.

3. The deep sleep of the body when one does not dream, but one is able to do astral travelling.

AVATAR or AVATARA: This is a very rare person nowadays. It is a person who has no Karma, a person who is not necessarily human, but one who adopts human form in order that humans may be helped. It is observed that an Avatar (male) or Avatara (female) is always higher than human.

In the Christian Bible you read of angels descending to the deepest hells of Earth in order that they may bring assistance to suffering humanity.

Avatars appear on those occasions when the world is in danger, or when humanity as a species is in danger. You may not recognise Avatars because they often have great suffering. They are pure, and unless they are able to take certain suffering they could not stay on the Earth. You can liken them to a deep-sea diver who has to put leaden weights upon his body that he may sink down into the depths of the dark and mysterious sea.

You will not recognise Avatars unless you are very pure, because the Avatar does not advertise his state on radio or television, nor does he tell you that if you take a certain magazine monthly you are sure of entry into the highest realms of Heaven!

AVESHA: This interesting condition means entering another's body. At times an Avatar will need to take possession of another's body in order to do some special work, but such possession is only accomplished when the original occupant of the body agrees. After some seven years, never more, the Avatar has changed everything in the body, every cell, every molecule, and so the body becomes truly his.

Two points of interest—some people say, 'Well, how can a molecule change places?' The answer is, of course, that even in the humble process of electro-plating, molecules are sent from one electrode to the other electrode of a plating vat. Thus, even a base metal can have pure gold deposited upon it.

The second point—often an Avatar will take over a body which is already adult. That is because the Avatar must not waste the time of being born and growing up through the painful stages of childhood.

AVIDYA: This is a form of ignorance. It is the mistake of regarding life on Earth as the only form of life that matters. Earth life is merely life in a classroom, the life beyond is the one that matters.

On other planets, in other universes, there are entities, some not so intelligent as humans, and some incredibly more intelligent than humans. They may not follow the human pattern of body form, but they are still sentient Beings.

B

BEYOND: This refers to the Great Beyond. It indicates that state of existence beyond the physical in which we find ourselves, it refers to life beyond the Vale of Death.

People throughout ages, and all over the world, have speculated on the nature of 'The Beyond.' It is unfortunate that so-called scientists want to weigh everything, test everything, and prove everything, because that limits their ability to perceive the obvious. When a person is ready to receive the truth, then the truth comes to him, and he knows the truth of that truth for that which is needs no proof, while that which is NOT cannot be proven.

BHAGAVAD GITA: This is one of the great Scriptures of India in which a truly enlightened Teacher teaches that which should not be altered. The eighteen chapters of this book each deal with one aspect of human life, and show how by using the physical, emotional, mental, ethical, and spiritual abilities of one's Ego at the same time one can attain to true harmony of body and spirit.

This book teaches that only through true harmony can Man progress into Divinity, and so obtain release from the wheel of birth, growth, death, and rebirth.

The actual meaning of the words are—Bhaga, the Sun. Vad means Godlike. Gita means Song.

BHAGAVAN. A term indicative of one's personal God. The God whom we worship irrespective of the name which we use, and in different parts of the world different names are used for the same God.

It is the God with six attributes, which are:

1. Power and dominion.
2. Might.
3. Glory.
4. Splendour.
5. Wisdom.
6. Renunciation.

BHAJAN: A form of worship of one's God through singing. It does not refer so much to spoken prayers, but is specifically related to singing. One can chant prayers, and that would be Bhajan.

An example of that in the Christian religion is the chanting of the Psalms.

BHAKTA: One who worships God, a follower of God. Again, it must be stressed that this can be any God, it does not relate to any particular creed or belief, but is a generic term.

BHAKTI: An act of devotion to one's God. The act of identifying oneself as a child of God, as a subject of God, and admitting that one is subservient and obedient to God.

BHAVA: This is being, feeling, existing, emotion. Among human beings there are three stages of Bhavas:

1. The pashu-bhava is the lowest group of people who live solely for themselves and for their own selfish pleasures. They think ill and do ill to others. They have no interest except in their own social or financial advantage, and they never help others in any way at all. They are the people on the lowest step of evolution.

2. The vira-bhava are the middle group. They have ambition and desire to progress upwards. They are strong, and frequently have quite a lot of energy. Unfortunately, they are selfish and domineering when they think someone might be getting more than they. They are the type who want to be 'Do-gooders,' not for the sake of helping others, but so that they shall be known as great and holy people always ready to assist those in need. Actually, it is very false policy to have anything to do with do-gooders, because they are selfish, egocentric people who have a long, long way to go.

3. This group, the divya-bhava, is of a much better type, with harmonising people who are thoughtful, unselfish, and really interested in helping others unselfishly. They will go to great

effort to help those who seek help, and they do not do it for self-gain.

Sadly enough, this group are very much in the minority at present.

BODHA: That knowledge which can be imparted to another person whom one is teaching. It is also referred to as wisdom or understanding.

One can teach a person from a textbook and a certain amount of knowledge will be absorbed parrot fashion, but the real knowledge comes by being 'rubbed off' from the teacher and passing to the pupil. It is knowledge acquired by copying the teacher.

BODHI: A Buddhist word which indicates that one has a clear appreciation of the nature of that which is beyond this life. It is perfect knowledge, it is perfect understanding, we in the flesh are mere figments of the Ego's imagination, formed for the purpose of gaining experience.

BRAHMA: A Hindu God frequently represented with four arms and four faces and holding various religious symbols. But there is another Brahma. Brahma—this is a state. It indicates that everything is in a stage where change is accomplished by the thought of all incarnate minds, minds which shape the present and the future, and it means 'to expand,' just as the experience of all living creatures constantly expands.

BRAHMACHARI: One who has taken the first monastic vows. Or it may be a spiritual person who is devoted to the observance and practises of a form of religion but as yet has taken no particular monastic vows.

BRAHMACHARYA: This is the fourth of the Abstinencies. The things enjoined on one by this are purity of thought, purity of word and deed, an initiation in which one takes vows, a celibate stage so that one may gain the necessary experience of astral travelling. It should be noted that the latter stage has four separate stages; the first of which is that in which the individual is governed by a Teacher.

BRAHMALOKA: This is that plane of existence where those who have succeeded in the Earth life go that they may commune with others in the next plane of existence. It is a stage where one lives in divine communication while meditating on and preparing for fresh experiences.

It is, in fact, a stage where one goes to the Hall of Memories and consults the Akashic Record that one may see what one has accomplished during the last life on Earth, and what has been left undone.

It is here that one is able to consult with those of great experience, so that one may plan one's next incarnation to remedy the defects of the last and to make a step farther in overcoming one's Karma.

BRAHMA-SUTRAS: All these words come from India, and the Brahma-Sutras are very famous aphorisms which place before one the principal Teachings of the Upanishads. The Upanishads will be dealt with under U and under V.

It is a sad fact that every translator and commentator, particularly in the Western world, injects his own opinions into his translations and commentaries, people are not content to merely translate. Thus it is that in the Brahma-Sutras one translation may not agree with another, and unless one can see the original by way of the Akashic Record one can be led sadly astray.

BREATH: One should also give it the name of Pranayama, but as this would mean nothing to the majority of people, let us be content with the word Breath.

There is a special supplement at the end of this Dictionary dealing with various systems of breathing, dealing with various exercises in the matter of breathing, so let us now state that breathing relates to the rhythm in which we take in air, hold it, and release it.

As an instance let us take one's own unit of time, and then have one unit of time for breathing in, four units of that time for retaining the breath, and two units of that time for exhaling. That is a comfortable breathing rhythm for inducing calmness.

As the unit of time one might take three seconds, so that we breathe in for three seconds, hold one's breath for three times four, that is, twelve seconds, and exhale for three times two, that is, six seconds.

It is strongly advised that you do not practise different systems of Yogic breathing until you know what you are doing, because until you have definite knowledge of what you are trying and why and what the results may be, you can endanger your health. The exercises given at the end of this Dictionary are quite, quite harmless, and are, in fact, really helpful.

BUDDHA: This is not a God, this is a person who has successfully completed the lives of a cycle of existence, and by his success in overcoming Karma is now ready to move on to another plane of existence.

A Buddha is a person who is free from the bonds of the flesh. The one who is frequently referred to as 'The Buddha' was actually Siddhartha Gautama. He was a Prince who lived some two thousand five hundred years ago in India; he renounced all material possessions in order to find enlightenment. He found Nirvana, which does not mean, as it usually translated, everything full of nothingness. We shall deal with Nirvana under the letter N.

Every one of us should strive to attain to Buddhahood which is a state of being, an exalted state of being. It is not a God.

Western people are often puzzled by 'The Thousand Buddhas.' They think that there are at least a thousand Gods, which, of course, is too fantastic to be even ridiculous!

Buddhahood is a state of being. One can attain Buddhahood no matter what one's station in life. The Prince or the garbage collector can each be pure and holy. Down on this Earth we are like actors on a stage, and we take the 'dess' or status which will be of most assistance to us in learning that which we have to learn. The Thousand Buddhas, then, is merely an indication that one can attain to Buddhahood in a thousand or so different ways.

Why the thousand? Well, think of a small boy who says, 'My father? Ah! He's got MILLIONS of 'em!' The thousand, then, is merely a figure of speech. Buddha is a symbol, not the graven image of a God. The Buddha figures are just reminders of what we can be if we want to be, and if we work to be.

BUDDHI: A word meaning wisdom, and we must always keep before us the awareness that wisdom and knowledge are quite different things. Wisdom comes with experience; knowledge can be obtained without the wisdom to apply that knowledge which we have gained. We have to attain to Buddhi, which is wisdom, before we can pass on to Buddhahood which is wisdom and knowledge.

BUDDHISM: Frequently people refer to Buddhism as a religion. Actually, it would be far more correct to say it is a Way of Life, a code of living, a manner of passing our time upon this Earth, so that we shall hurt none and advance our own spiritual progress in the quickest time with the least effort.

Here are various things which one must do, and various

things which one must not do. The Buddhists refer to (1) as The Four Noble Truths:

1. There is suffering and there is a cause for that suffering. Suffering can be overcome, and then there is a way of peace.

2. Nirvana. Mind and matter are in a state of constant change. The mind causes the spirit to bog down as if stuck in clay. Withdraw the mind, and then one attains to Nirvana and so becomes free from suffering and the cycle of continual rebirth, living, dying, and being reborn.

3. The Eightfold Path, which means—

> Correct views.
> Correct aspirations.
> Correct speech.
> Correct conduct.
> Correct methods of livelihood.
> Correct effort.
> Correct thoughts.
> Correct contemplation.

As in most religions, or ways of life, there are different branches. Just as the Christian Religion has a whole horde of different branches from the Plymouth Brethren to the Roman Catholic faith, so does the Buddhist school branch into two—they are The Hinayana, which means the Narrow Way, and The Mahayana, which means the Great Way. The former is rather austere, it has a narrow outlook, it relates to the achievement of personal sanctity through seclusion and aesthetism. This is indeed a rigorous living.

The latter, Mahayana, prefers to follow the precepts of Gautama Buddha as a divine incarnation.

One might say that one of these calls upon a person to progress by his own efforts, while the other says that you can only work and progress by following the precise and undeviating example of another.

C

CAUSAL BODY: For those who love big words this is the Anandamaya-kosha, or, if you prefer it under yet a different language instead of in simple, plain language, you could term it the Karana Sharira.

The causal body is the first of the various bodies with which we are encumbered. Think of us as being a nest of boxes, one inside the other, or think of us as anything which fits one inside the other; it could be a collection of those small coffee tables, or boxes, or a nest of drawers, anything which has a small subject, then a larger outside and a larger outside that, and so on. This is how our different bodies are arranged.

The causal body is the innermost one, and it is that which commences the processes whereby we gain experiences in the flesh. This, the causal body, is the body of incarnation, and it is the one which causes all those familiar troubles associated with the flesh—lusts of various kinds, numerous exciting desires, horrible greed, and, the most common of all, selfishness.

We have to live so that there is no need for us to have a causal body, because when we can manage without a causal body we do not have to come back to this Earth nor go to other material and unpleasant worlds.

CHAITANYA: A state when the spiritual consciousness has just been awakened, and one is alert and ready to progress upwards, taking the first steps to leave the causal body behind one.

To attain to Chaitanya means hard work, hard study, constant meditation and contemplation. When the conditions are right, the six Chakras are stimulated and come into consciousness, giving one awareness of one's destiny, giving an understanding of what must be before one can progress speedily.

CHAKRAS: We should concentrate upon the six Chakras. Along our spine, like wheels threaded along our spinal column, are the six man Chakras or centres of psychic consciousness. There are various centres which keep our causal body in touch with our higher bodies, in touch with our higher centres.

Some people prefer to call these Chakras, Lotuses. Others call them Wheels. Some religions make a stylised symbol which one can recognise as a Wheel or as a Lotus, depending upon one's poetic imagination.

There are six Chakras along the spine, and a seventh in the centre of the cerebrum. There are two others making nine in all, but most people have not attained to the state yet where they can assimilate knowledge of nine, so let us deal only with the orthodox and commonly accepted seven.

When one can see the aura, one can see all the colours swirling out from these different Chakras, and, of course, the colours and the auric emanations of all types are different between man and woman.

The first Chakra is at the base of the spine near the excretory organ. The second is at the genitalia level, the third is at the umbilicus, the fourth approximates to the level of the heart, the fifth comes at the level of the throat, and the sixth is at the eyebrow level.

Mythology states that the lower man dwells in the lowest part of the spine, and not until Man is able to raise the Kundalini powers into the heart Chakra is he able to be aware of progress. Man has to send his spiritual forces into the sixth Chakra before being able to make any really satisfactory progress, and when one can get above the seventh then one knows quite surely that one is living on Earth for the last time.

CHAN: This now means meditation. It is a word used by the Japanese Zen Buddhists.

Originally the word was Channa, and it then signified that the person concerned had experienced instantaneous perception of Truth. You might say that the person who had Channa had experienced a revelation.

CHANG: The opposite of artificial, the opposite of abnormal. That which is completely normal, completely standard. It is a word from the Chinese Taoist belief.

CHANISM: A theory whereby one can attain to the state of Buddhahood through sudden enlightenment, through a sudden lightning flash of revelation.

Devotees of Chanism engage in constant meditation upon the principles and precepts of the Eternal Truths in the hope of receiving this sudden revelation.

CHARMS: Many people look upon charms as idle superstitions, they look upon charms as little ornaments which the gullible buy in the hope of changing their luck. Well, if you go to some souvenir shop and buy a charm it is just the same as throwing your money away. But if you have a specially prepared charm, prepared, that is, by a person who knows how to do it, the charm is effective.

It means that one has to build a thought form and locate it in the charm in much the same way as the Egyptians of old safeguarded their embalmed Pharaohs.

We shall deal with this more under Talismans.

CHENG: The honesty and sincerity inherent in one's true self. One has to allow Cheng to grow and to reveal itself before one can make any substantial progress.

If we cut away greed, lust, and selfishness like taking away the hard shell from a nut, we can get to the kernel inside. Humans are encased in a hard shell, and they have to shed that shell before they can progress.

CHI: This is vital force. Anything which comes within the sphere of matter. So we have Chi, the breath force which corresponds on the lowest plane with the etheric force, and then, higher, with the auric force.

CHIT: Consciousness, a rather empty sort of consciousness. It is a lack of any specific awareness. One might say that it is being conscious without having any specific purpose to that consciousness, without learning anything through that consciousness.

CHITTA: This is the lower mind. There are three parts of the mind, or it might be better to say mind-stuff. The first is Manas; the second is Buddhi; and the third is Ahamkara. The first, of course, is the lowest.

Everything which comes into the lower mind passes into the sub-conscious for storage and sorting, and possibly for later use. It should be remembered that within our sub-conscious we have the knowledge of all humanity, but through imperfections we have very imperfect memories, that is, we cannot get down to all the knowledge we have.

CHOICE: It is unfortunate that in this world people try to influence others. Christians, for example, try to influence non-Christians to change religions or change beliefs. It seems that a person of a certain belief is not at all sure of his beliefs, and so he must try to persuade others to the same belief in the hope that it will mean that in numbers there is safety.

It is wrong to influence one's free choice of the Path of life and spirituality. If a person is always wanting proof, then that person should be let be. It means that the person is not ready to take a particular Path.

To compel a person to take a certain Path against his or her will is useless, it merely adds to the Karma of the person compelling and does no good to anyone. So, all you who are do-gooders, remember that in trying to influence the Path of another, or in trying to compel conversion, you are harming yourself.

CITY OF NINE GATES: Many occult or metaphysical books refer to the City of Nine Gates. It is a device to thwart those who try to scan through occult literature without having a genuine interest, without having a genuine knowledge of the subject. It is a device to blind the superficial, the unevolved, and the merely curious.

The City of Nine Gates, of course, is the physical body which has nine main openings, two eyes, two ears, two nostrils, etc. The other openings need not be detailed, as you should know them.

Through each of the nine gates can come enemies which will stultify one's progress. For example, a very good man can be tempted by 'the enemy' entering through his eyes; he may see some sight which stimulates his wrong desires, desires which he thought he had overcome. He might find 'the enemy' entering through his nostrils, so that there would be scents which would unduly disturb his greed senses. It must be stated, however, that it is also possible to progress very satisfactorily through the use instead of the misuse of the nine gates.

CLAIRVOYANCE: True clairvoyance means that one's astral body can get out of the physical body, and can then 'see' in dimensions which cannot be contacted while in the physical body.

The average person can see physically only those things which are within the range of his eyesight; he may look about a room and see a chair, a table, and a wall, but that which is in the room beyond is also beyond his sight. In clairvoyance one can see through the wall as if there were no wall, or as if, in those of lesser ability, a vague grey mist was there instead.

When one gets into the astral stage one can consult the Akashic Record and see any incident which has happened, or any incident which is happening. One can also see the probabilities for the future, that is, one can see that a person is going to have good fortune or bad fortune.

Clairvoyance can be developed, it is the right of men and women, and before men and women became so selfish and used powers for their own gain everyone was clairvoyant.

CONCENTRATION: This is the act of devoting one's full attention to one thing, it may be a physical thing or an intangible thing, such as an idea.

One should concentrate along certain fixed rules, which means that one's attention should be focused strongly upon the object on which one desires to concentrate.

As an illustration, consider a candle. Have a lighted candle before you, sit in any position which is comfortable, and think about that candle, think about it as you gaze vaguely in its direction, but without actually seeing the candle.

What does the candle look like? Is there any smell to it? How was it made? What is the nature of the flame? How is the flame sustained? And if the candle is burning, and matter is stated to be indestructible, what happens to the candle when it is going up in flames? If you think upon these lines you can greatly develop your powers of concentration.

In Tibet a monk will concentrate with a burning stick of incense upon his head, he has to maintain his concentration even when the burning incense starts to scorch the skin of his shaven skull. A monk in attendance will, of course, remove the incense before any harm is done, but the student monk must not remove it; if he does it shows that his concentration is not sufficient.

CONTEMPLATION: Contemplation often takes over when meditation ends. One may be meditating upon a certain subject and then one may find that one has come to the end of the information concerning the matter upon which one was meditating. Then contemplation takes over.

One can contemplate upon the beauty of the setting sun, or one can contemplate upon the reason for the particular or peculiar action of a person.

Contemplation is basically of two types:

1. Cognitive, in which a material object or matter is thought about. *Or.*

2. Non-cognitive, in which one dwells upon things of the spirit, things beyond Man's material perception, but one has to be particularly evolved, particularly spiritually mature, before one can engage in non-cognitive contemplation.

CULT: Often a person of little knowledge, or of poor spiritual perception will imagine that he or she is a Great Teacher, and will then by propaganda get a small group of people to whom he or she will expound the great truth which has been received by this method or that method, or direct voice, or automatic writing, or something else.

It is tragic that often these groups distort the Great Truths. They merely exist to pander to the exalted ideas of some person who has barely started on The Path. One should only enter a group or cult when one is quite sure that one is doing right.

There are enough orthodox religions—Jewish, Christian, Buddhist, or whatever you like—without all these subsidiary cults springing up.

All too often a cult is started as a money-making device preying upon the gullible. While one must agree that a Teacher needs to have money that food and clothing may be bought, yet when the 'Teacher' uses his or her name as a basis for getting members, or when he or she stresses that the Teacher is the important thing, you may be sure that there is something wrong; the name of a Teacher does not matter, all that matters is what does the Teacher teaches. Is it good? Does it satisfy your needs? Does it require that you pay large sums of money before you go on to the next meeting or the next lesson? If so, be careful, it may be a money-making racket.

If you are in doubt why not see a priest of the religion to which you were born? If you are sufficiently determined you can see a higher priest of the religion to which you were born. But it is desired here to issue a solemn warning against cults which purport to teach all sorts of magic, purport to give all sorts of demonstrations, but only if you pay enough. Remember, it may be your mental health which suffers.

D

DAMA: This is a word which relates to the quietening of the ten organs of sense and action, for it is obvious that until one can quieten one's sense and action perceptions one cannot adequately meditate or contemplate. Attaining to Dama is one of the Six Attainments, and that will be referred to under the letter S.

DEATH: This, in the occult sense, is the severing of the Silver Cord, which parts the astral body or Soul from the physical body.

There is nothing to be afraid of in death, because death is as natural as birth. Death, in fact, is the process of being reborn into another plane of existence.

It is a provision of nature that people normally are afraid to die. There is an ingrained racial fear of death, and that is necessary because if people knew how simple dying really is there would be more suicides, and that would be a bad thing because as soon as a suicide gets to the other side of death the poor fellow gets shoved back into another body—as a baby, of course—and then he has to live for his allotted span.

Every person coming to Earth has his days numbered, that is, his time of birth is known and his time of death is known. Thus, if a person commits suicide he gets put into the body of a baby and is sent back to Earth, and if he only had a few months to live, then he might be born again stillborn; if he had two or three years to live, then the baby would die at two or three years.

Death is a good thing. It would be intolerable to think that one lived on this benighted Earth for eternity. Death is release from the toils of Earth, it enables one to evolve and to educate our Overself.

DEHA: This actually means 'One who has a body.' Man has three basic bodies, the dense, the subtle or not so dense, and the causal, but we will deal with that more extensively under the letter U.

The body is the means whereby the immortal Soul or Overself can gain experience from a physical life. The body is merely an instrument or puppet. You may like to read more about this under the letter P—Planes of Existence.

DEITY: Scriptures of all kinds state 'Thou shalt not worship graven images.' But to have a picture or an image of some sacred, revered figure, is not necessarily to worship a graven image. The image reminds one of that which one can become provided one tries hard enough. Similarly, a sacred picture or a sacred image to which one is attached can act as a very sound point of focus when one engages in meditation or contemplation. That is why some people have a personal Shrine at home with perhaps a photograph or an image or some picture—it acts as a soothing influence which puts one into the right frame of mind.

One can train one's mind to think of the sacred object to the exclusion of more mundane articles. Sacred pictures or sacred images are acceptable and permissible provided they are used as reminders and not as objects of senseless worship.

It must be pointed out that Christians use a Crucifix not necessarily as an object of worship, but as an object of reminding.

DEVA: A Deva is a Divine Being, one who is quite beyond the human state. Anyone who has attained to the necessary degree of enlightenment and purity, and is no longer on this Earth, could be a Deva.

Nature Spirits and manmade thought forms are not, and cannot ever be Devas of the human type, although naturally Nature Spirits and Animal Spirits have their own Group-Devas.

DEVILS: These people are the negative of the positive of good. It follows that if there were no devils there would be no Gods! If we have a positive we must have a negative otherwise the positive could not exist. If you have a battery you cannot have just a positive terminal because no current would flow, you must have a negative terminal as well in order to complete the circuit.

Devils are necessary and they do quite a lot of good; they remind one that it is much better to be on the side of good than fall into the clutches of devils, who are alleged to be quite unkind. Actually, there is a very real Force of Evil. Evil is a potent, tangible force. I look upon good and bad as something like trying to climb up some very, very steep hill in a car; the hill is so steep that you have to be in bottom gear all the time, and you are afraid that your engine is going to stop and your brakes won't hold, and so back you will go.

However, that is a personal thought. Let it be stated as a fact that evil and devils are necessary because otherwise there would be no incentive to good, there would, in fact, be no yardstick by which we could measure good.

DHANURASANA: Some people for peculiar reasons of their own seem to like to try different postures. Although I have never seen the slightest use of these, here is one which you may want to try if you feel you should do a doctor or chiropractor a good turn. Make sure that you or your relatives know his telephone number before you start.

This Dhanurasana is a Yogic Posture sometimes termed the Bow Posture. If you really want to try it, lie on the ground with your face down, bring your legs backwards towards your neck so that your hands can catch hold of your ankles. Then pull yourself together so that your head and chest are off the ground.

Pull harder so that your legs and most of your thighs also are off the ground. Then you are teetering rather absurdly on a somewhat vulnerable part of your anatomy. Try this a few times, and afterwards try to decide what is the sense of it. It should be observed here that one can be good—one can be very good—without all these gymnastic contortions which are merely an exhibitionist stunt.

DHARMA: This word can indicate merit, good morals, righteousness, truth, or a way of life. Its true meaning, however, is 'that which holds your true nature.'

It means that one should take a way of life and maintain that way of life, without slipping back from the high standards which one has previously set oneself.

In Buddhism, Dharma means following the Noble Eight-fold Path.

DHAUTIS: This is a word meaning cleansing. For a Western person it is a very dangerous process indeed, and should never, never, never be carried out except under the closest supervision of one who has been trained to a very high standard and knows the harm that can be caused if it is done carelessly.

Dhautis is a system of purification of the physical body, and does not confer any psychic abilities. Certain people in India swallow air and expel it forcibly in various unusual ways. Afterwards they swallow water and expel that in the same unusual ways.

Some of the practitioners of this in India swallow a strip of cloth, securely holding one end, of course. They swallow the other end of the cloth until a very considerable length is in the stomach. Then they rub and pound the stomach, afterwards pulling out the cloth, to which adhere all sorts of things from the stomach and throat.

Another stage is when the person passes a thread through the nostrils and brings it out through the mouth. The thread is pulled backwards and forwards in much the same way as one would clean a chimney.

This should be left well alone, and it is mentioned here so that you have been warned to leave it well alone.

DHYANA: This is a meditation or a deep form of concentration. It is an unbroken flow of thought towards that upon which one concentrates. It is a word which in Raja Yoga is known as the Seventh of the Eight Limbs.

DIET: Diet usually relates to food, although there is such a thing as a spiritual diet. But using this to refer to food it may be stated that many people have all sorts of weird ideas about diet. Some are strictly vegetarian, some eat meat. My own view is that at the present stage Man is a meat-eating animal, so if you feel the need for meat—eat meat.

32

One should not over-eat, one should eat in order to live, and not live in order to eat. If one is doing occult study, garlic and anything bitter or acid should be avoided.

Diet is just a common-sense approach to what one should eat. Do not eat too much, do not drink anything intoxicating because to do so is to desecrate the Temple of the Soul and to drive the astral body out of the physical body. Unfortunately, the stage into which the astral body is driven is known as the lower astral, which can be decidedly unpleasant.

Many people are fervent vegetarians, they will not eat meat because they think that some animal has to be killed. Well, why will these people cure an illness? Germs or virus are animals of a certain type, and to cure an illness you have to kill the germs, and how do you know that a cabbage has no feeling? Russian scientists have come up with a suggestion that all vegetables have feeling. The best way, if you feel that you should be a faddist and refrain from eating anything which has to be killed, is to starve, because you might accidentally bite a lettuce with feeling.

DIKSHA: This is the act of initiating a student into spiritual life, and is carried out by the Teacher or Guru concerned.

It might be worth mentioning here that the Teacher or Guru really is the one who should say when an initiation is carried out. From personal experience it may be stated that students always overrate their own abilities, whether spiritual or otherwise.

DIMENSIONS: People talk about the fourth dimension, or the fifth dimension, and beyond. People say that we are upon a three-dimensional world. Unfortunately, it is not possible to discuss the fourth, fifth, sixth, seventh, eighth, or ninth dimension to a person living in a third-dimensional existence.

We cannot be content with this, however, so let us put ourselves in the position of a one-dimensional person.

A one-dimensional being could only exist upon a line. If you draw the thinnest line that you possibly can on a piece of paper, and you imagine that one particle of graphite from your pencil is a person living on that one-dimensional world, and then remember that that piece of graphite is our person. Our person, then, lives on that line, and that line is the whole universe to that person. If you make one end of the line A, and the other end B, you will see that the person can progress from A, which is birth, to B, which is death. The person will be able to move torwards only, they cannot move backwards because that would be moving into the past.

Supposing that you could place a point, or perhaps a finger, on that thin line, then the person in that one-dimensional world would see phenomena in its sky. It would see only that part of your finger actually in contact with the line, and it would be impossible to visualise what you looked like, in that same way as it is impossible for most people in this three-dimensional world of ours to visualise what is behind the so-called 'flying saucer.'

If we go on to a two-dimensional world what would we have? It would be a plane surface, and the inhabitants would have to be flat figures. Now supposing you draw a line around one of these figures, it would prove to be a barrier to him because the line will have thickness, and to a completely flat person height would be beyond his understanding. If he tried to climb up that pencil line—which to him, of course, would be a considerable height—it would be the same as going out into space.

Our flat being would not be able to look down on the line and see that it was comparatively flat. Thus a line or an angle would be an astounding phenomena to a flat being.

By the way, just try this if you doubt what I am saying: Hold a pencil at a level with your eyes so that the pencil is lengthwise to you. Then behind it hold another pencil end on. You will not be able to see that pencil because it will be hidden by the line of the first pencil. Thus you will be in the position of our flat being, and before you can see the second pencil you will have to enter another dimension, that is, you will have to descend below the level of the pencils or rise above it, so that you can look up or down and see by perspective.

The fourth dimension is actually where we have travelled into the astral, because we then have different abilities, and although we can fully exist, although we do exist, we cannot be seen by people of third dimension except as a ghost.

DIRECT COGNITION: This is full realisation, awareness of that which cannot be taught. One cannot have a full realisation of the fourth dimension or of what our Overself is like while we are in the body, nor can another person necessarily convince us of anything connected with this, nor with a God. We have to know by direct cognition, by direct realisation.

DISASSOCIATION: Some people have a loose astral body,

and when the person in the flesh goes day-dreaming he or she may separate into physical and astral.

Some years ago there was a case in France where an unfortunate schoolteacher, a woman, had this remarkable ability that when she was engrossed in a subject her physical and spiritual bodies parted. It created a lot of alarm in her pupils when they could see two teachers, apparently twins. Eventually it came to the knowledge of the school authorities and the schoolteacher became a schoolteacher no more.

Disassociation can also relate to a mental state in which a person is not able to control mental processes.

DISEMBODIED : When we do astral travelling we are in the disembodied state, that is, our astral becomes disassociated from the physical and we are connected only by the Silver Cord.

When we are thinking of ourselves, we are in the embodied state, that is, the embodied state is a temporary thing and endures only for our stay on Earth.

The disembodied state means what it says—out of the body; we have to get out of the body to know what we are, what we are doing, and where we are going.

DIVINITY : This is one of the very old original Sanskrit words. It goes back to the earliest days of Mankind. It means 'to shine.' Often a Deva or a Godlike person will be known as 'The Shining One.'

In connection with this, you may be interested to remember that when Moses descended from the mountain his face was shining and he had to veil his face so that the shining light was obscured from the common gaze.

DREAMS : One of the most misunderstood subjects of all. Because of Western Man's conditioning Western Man can rarely believe in astral travelling and such things, thus it is that when the astral body rejoins the physical body complete with a lot of most interesting memories, the physical body rejects the story and alters it to fit the facts which are acceptable to Western training. Thus a person who has met another in the astral world and discussed various courses of action, will say in the morning, 'Oh, I dreamed of So-and-So last night. He was in a bad temper. Wonder what it means?'

Some dreams, of course, can be caused by eating too much and too richly before going to bed, but that is a mere disturbance of the body functions and cannot be taken seriously. In this case the lower mind and the emotional mind get together and set aside the reasoning part of the mind. One should write down one's so-called 'dreams' immediately one awakens, because if that is done conscientiously one soon reaches the stage when one is able to recall the actual astral travelling experience which occasioned the mis-called 'dream.'

DWAPARAYUGA: Throughout the world in world religions there are various systems which divide the life of this world into different periods or cycles. According to Hindu mythology the world is divided into four stages, each of 864,000 years.

The four periods become successively more evil. In the first period right and good prevails, but with each period the power of evil increases, the power of wrong-doing increases.

At present we are in the fourth stage, the stage of Kali, and no doubt everyone will agree that the world at present is an evil place in which those of bad intentions invariably get the upper hand, a stage in which treachery succeeds.

When this cycle has ended the world will start again on a new cycle where goodness will predominate. But in the Age of Kali, of course, there must be some 'Saviour' who will start and set the world right. That is the unvarying process.

DWESHA: This is aversion, dislike as opposed to like. It goes back into the memory department. If we have had a severe shock we dislike that which caused the shock, and we try to avoid getting such shocks in the future.

We may not be aware of that which caused the shock because it may have been pushed down into our sub-conscious and a form of amnesia will have taken over to block the unpleasant memory.

In the process of Analysis the practitioner helps one to delve down into the sub-conscious memory to dredge up the unpleasant occurrences, so that having seen the cause of behaviour one can realise that cause, and avoid such behaviour patterns in the future.

E

EGO: This indicates that part of one which is conscious of 'I.' It is the separate individuality apart from the Overself. There are two kinds of Ego; the first is that which is learning willingly or unwillingly. It is undeveloped, untutored, excessively talkative, over-confident without any reason to be confident. That

Ego is self-centred, arrogant, and aggressive. It is, in fact, the typical Man In The Street.

The other Ego is one which has progressed and has learned by experience. It is possessed by those who have attained to much enlightenment. It is a person who is willing to help others even at the risk of inconvenience and trouble for oneself.

Egoism is often referred to as the second of the five sources of trouble, and when one thinks of conceited, egotistical people whom we know, we can well understand that this is so. Unfortunately, the less one knows the more one thinks one knows. Many of these people who are so boastful, who say, 'Prove this, prove that, and I don't believe it anyhow,' have not even started to learn.

It is believed by this writer that few Press people are in the developed category, because one of the first requirements is that an Ego cannot be developed unless it is willing to consider the feelings and needs of others—a matter singularly lacking with Press people.

ELEMENTALS: Most people are horribly confused about elementals. Actually elementals are a type of thought form which have a sort of half-life of their own, a form of life brought into being by humans.

So that one may the more easily understand it, let us say that we have a magnet and the magnet represents the human. Then let us say that we bring the magnet near a piece of iron. Immediately, the iron becomes magnetised to some lesser degree, and so it represents the elemental.

Elementals are formed from the etheric substance which was the origin of all complex forms. All the random thoughts of people 'magnetise' etheric substances which give rise to elementals—elementary beings.

It should be made clear that many people who go to seances and believe that they have conversed with the spirit of dear departed Aunt Matilda, have really been the victim of a hoax by some elementals. Elementals are irresistibly drawn to seances because it gives them a chance to play a joke on humans. Elementals are as mischievous as monkeys, and possibly even more brainless than monkeys.

One of the great dangers of going to seances is that one may be completely deluded by these thought forms.

In addition to the elementals, of course, there are Nature Spirits, but that will be dealt with under N.

ELEMENTS: There are, of course, quite a number of elements, but to the occultist, the metaphysician, or the astrologer, there are five main elements. They are ether, air, fire, water, and earth. We are not dealing with chemistry here but with astrological lore.

These elements come into play to a very great extent in astrology, where one can be born under a watery sign—Cancer—and then if one marries a person who was born under a fiery sign, such as Aries, there can be trouble and an unhappy marriage because fire and water do not mix. It is a question of that which is compatible and that which is not compatible.

The elements are important things indeed for those who want to study the mechanics of metaphysics.

EMOTION: Emotion is a state of mind which should be controlled so that it does not interfere with one's metaphysical studies. It is easy to imagine that one has seen a ghost or that one has spoken to a person who has recently left this Earth. It is also possible that emotion—fear—will prevent us from doing just that.

In esoteric work one must curb, and train, and restrain the emotions. One must not be too sceptical, and one must not be too willing to accept, one must use common-sense.

One must keep a balanced mind and be ready to investigate all matters with an open mind. By open mind, is meant the state where one is not going to condemn and one is not going to believe unless there are reasonable grounds for either state.

The Middle Way is the best way, so that one is not too credulous nor too incredulous. By taking a middle of the road path one is able to see the scenery on each side, and judge accordingly.

ENTHUSIASM: This is one of the things about which one has to be very careful. One must keep one's enthusiasm and one's emotion under control. One must not become excessively enthusiastic. To become over-enthusiastic about a thing disturbs the even tenor of one's existence.

We have a certain amount of energy, and if we allot too much energy to one subject then we have not enough energy to deal with other subjects, and we become unbalanced.

In Yogic or metaphysical matters there should be no excitement, no false enthusiasm, and no strong emotions. Here again the only way to attain to a sound balance is to take the Middle Way.

ETHERIC DOUBLE: This is the substance existing between the physical body and the aura. The etheric is of a bluish-grey colour, and is not substantial like flesh and bone. The etheric can pass through a brick wall, leaving both intact.

The etheric double is the absolute counterpart of the human flesh and blood body, but in etheric form. The stronger a person's physical, the stronger will be the etheric. When a person dies, and that person has had a certain gross interest in life, his etheric double is physically very strong and he leaves a ghost which, through habit, acts in precisely the same way as the person did while in the physical body.

A person who has been killed by violence or in a state of terror will have a very strong etheric indeed. People who have died by violence will often leave a ghost which can be seen.

Frequently disembodied etheric doubles try to dissipate their useless energy by going to seances and giving senseless messages. It is clear that if Uncle Timothy has died and Aunt Matilda wants to get in touch with him, she will go to a seance and, because of personal magnetism, she will attract the stupid etheric double of Uncle Timothy. This etheric double has no knowledge but only habits, and so it will react in much the same way as Uncle Timothy did on the Earth and will just give senseless information because it has no brain to direct it.

The etheric double is a useless thing which has to be dissipated before one is completely free of the bonds of Earth. It is the stuff of which senseless ghosts are made.

A person who is said to be earthbound is linked to Earth by this strong etheric double.

EVOLUTION: Everything is in a state of evolution. A child is born as a helpless baby, and gradually evolves into an adult. People go to school, and their evolution is such that they progress from class to class.

Men do not become angels on the earthly stage of evolution any more than animals turn into humans on this world. All must evolve according to the plans of the Universe, and according to their own species.

The development of Man, or Mankind, has been proceeding for many millions of years. By consulting the Akashic Record you will be able to see that the first form of Man was a globe, a creature not altogether solid, not altogether gaseous, something like an unpleasant murky sort of jelly. He had only one eye and no mind; instead, he was almost an automaton.

That was in the first Race of Man. In the second Race there was a difference because certain appendages protruded from the globe which was Man, and there was a rudimentary mind much as in the case of a monkey.

In the third Race of Man there was a dividing of the globe or sphere so that there were two sexes, male and female.

You may be interested in some of the different Races: In the first case with which we need deal there was the Race of the people of Lemuria, yes, there really was Lemuria! The Race at that time had instinct and passion, but they were not possessed of many of the higher emotions, not possessed of aspiration for spiritual pursuits.

The Earth in those days was still in a stage of development. Great gouts of flame shot out from the interior and there were earthquakes, and the Continent of Lemuria sank beneath the waves.

After the Lemurian Race there came the Atlantian Race. This was a definite improvement on the Lemurian because the Atlantian functioned on the higher emotions, they tried to develop their higher emotions, but they also evolved into a more reasoning type of mind, they went in for science a lot and, sadly, they produced an atom bomb thousands and thousands of years ago. The atom bomb went off, and the land called Atlantis sank beneath the waves. There were survivors scattered in various remote districts; some of their children were affected by radiations, and so there were mutations, mutations which caused the Aryan Race.

The Aryan Race is more of a concrete mind than spiritual, in fact, trying to get spiritual thoughts into most people is like trying to break concrete!

A sixth Race is functioning in the abstract, and eventually in the age of Aquarius, into which we are now entering, they will evolve into a spiritual mind. After this spiritual development we shall have a greater incursion into the abilities of a seventh Race. There are some of the seventh Race already on Earth, not many of them, but enough to provide a seed or nucleus, and the seventh Race will eventually achieve a knowledge of the leaders of this whole Solar System.

Evolution, then, is that which enables people, or anything, to develop and make progress.

EXPERIENCES: Many people during their time upon Earth have 'experiences.' They imagine they see things, or they actually do see things. They could be surer if they kept more accurate reports.

One should keep paper and pencil about at all times, particularly by the side of one's bed, so that if one is awakened notes can be made before the memory fades.

Supposing you are awakened in the night, and you think you see something. Make a note:

1. What did you see?
2. Was it male or female?
3. How was it dressed, in what period clothing?
4. What did it do? Did it come through a wall and stand by your bed?
5. What did it say or indicate to you?
6. What was your reaction?
7. What happened to the figure? Did it disappear—vanish —or go through a wall?
8. Having read the above, what conclusions can be formed? Was it hallucination? Was it a person that I recognised? Was it a person who appeared real?

In the morning read your notes, and then you can add to them anything which came from your sub-conscious in the night. It must be explained again, though, that many really authentic cases of visitations are lost to the world because the person who saw the visitor either dived beneath the bedclothes or was too confused to have any accurate memories. There are such things as ghosts, but if a person would not harm one when in the flesh, why should that person harm one when out of the flesh?

EYES: Everyone knows what eyes are, but the purpose of including that word here is so that we can deal with relaxation of the eyes, because eyes are among the most ill-used organs of the body.

It is essential that during meditation the eyes must not be strained. Most people focus their eyes on some imaginary object, or even upon some actual object. This is definitely harmful because it tires the eyes by requiring that the eye muscles remain in a fixed position.

One should look into the far distance, look beyond infinity so that the eye muscles are not being strained. You can, if you wish, relax your eyes by letting them wander, but, naturally, not while meditating. Let them wander so that the muscles are put in varying positions, and thus are not in any one position long enough to become tired or strained.

A good eye-massage exercise is to put the palms of one's hands over the eyes, and then move the hands slightly in order to form a cup. That is, when you pull out the palm of the hand while keeping the edge of the hand around the eye socket, you form a hollow with lessened air pressure.

If one presses on the eye's bony frame and then slightly eases away the palm, one can feel slight tension on the eyeball because the air pressure enables the liquid in the eye to push the eye out a bit. Then when you press in you get the opposite effect, and so you have a really relaxing eye massage.

F

FA: This is from the Chinese and it denotes the law or regulations. It indicates that one must follow the right precepts if one is going to make right progress. Until you can progress you will have to keep coming back to this dreary old world.

FACE: Look at the average person, look at the lines and wrinkles on their face, look at their tense, screwed-up expression! And when they think they are meditating they become screwed-up all the more. This is unfortunate because one cannot meditate when one is tense.

If you find that your face is becoming stiff, try relaxing it. Bend forward so that your face is parallel with the floor, make sure that the muscles of the face are quite slack, as slack as you can make them. See, also, that your lips are not tightly compressed, you can have your mouth slightly open if you prefer.

The eyes should be either very slightly open or shut, but you must not shut them tightly because if you do you are tensing muscles.

Relax the whole face, and then imagine that you are a dog who has just come out of the water sopping wet. Shake your head sharply as a dog does, so that even your ears waggle and your hair-do comes undone. Do that several times, pretend there is water on your face and you have to shake it off with sharp movements. Do this, and it really will shake out folds in your muscles.

When you have done this several times sit up straight, and stretch your neck as far up as you can. Imagine that you are a giraffe or one of those native tribeswomen who put rings on the neck in order that the neck may be lengthened.

When you have stretched your head as far up as you can, pull it down to your shoulders as far as you can, pull it right down into your shoulders so that your neck really is compressed. Stretch up your head again, and make it come down again. Do it several times, and every third time shake your head sharply like a dog does. This will help you more than you imagine.

FAITH: We must have faith if we are going to seek after knowledge because some things require that we have faith while we are still seeking for proof, and if a person goes seeking for a thing determined that they will not find it, then they will not find it.

It is wise to hold firm to the conviction that based upon intellectual ability we can ascertain that the thing under discussion is true.

In faith we try to prove that a thing is right, not, as so many do at present, try to prove that a thing is false.

Faith is no idle, senseless, ignorant belief. Faith grows and grows as one explores that in which one has faith.

FEAR: One of the greatest dangers in any form of occult study is of being afraid. In the East teachers tell the pupil, 'Fear not for there is naught to fear but fear.'

Fear corrodes our abilities for clear perception. If we are not afraid, nothing whatever can hurt us or disturb us. Therefore—fear not.

It is worth particularly noting that when one is doing astral travel there is no need for fear. Elementals or astral entities cannot hurt one, but if we are afraid, well, our fear upsets us—upsets our digestion, for instance. Again, let it be stated that no one can be harmed in the astral except by oneself, that is by getting frightened and rushing back with such a thunk that one becomes disassociated from the body.

If you come back into the body with a shocking jerk and get a headache after it, the remedy is simple—rest again and go to sleep, so that your astral body can leave the physical and resettle in the correct location in the physical body.

FO CHIAO: This is a Chinese interpretation of the Buddhist religion. As we have already stated, Buddhism is a code of living, a way of living, but in order to follow common usage it is referred to here as a religion.

Fo Chiao is the Chinese name for Buddhism as a religion.

FO HSUEH: This is Buddhist learning, Buddhism when treated as a philosophy or way of life, instead of as a religion. Again, it is from the Chinese concepts.

FORCES: There are four forces which need concern us. They are:

1. Natural forces: When we are at school we study a group of forces known as physics, or, if you prefer—heat, light, sound, electricity, and magnetism—and then one gets quite a dislike of poor old Pythagoras who worked out those weird and wonderful theorums which cause one so much trouble.

2. The etheric forces: Among these is included the power of the Kundalini. Those of the second group are still connected to natural phenomena because the Kundalini, and all that it implies, gets only as far as the etheric double before becoming a metaphysical force instead of an earth-natural force.

3. The ancient Egyptian priests specialised in this, which we might term 'Force 3.' They protected their tombs with thought-forms which really could make one frightfully uncomfortable.

Force 3 consists of all those things which are generated from the mind, and which, once generated, go on and on perhaps for centuries, until they have dissipated their original energy.

While this third force is still connected with nature, it is on a much more remote basis because we are now two stages removed from the crude, basic, natural force.

4. This is a force which can be generated by living entities because of the power of love, hate, etc. They are quite as powerful as are any of the preceding three.

Telepathy, clairvoyance, psychometry, levitation, teleportation, etc., come under this group.

Astral travelling does not come under this force, because astral travelling is just releasing the astral body from imprisonment in the physical body.

FOUR FRUITS: According to various Eastern beliefs, the Four Fruits of human life are that each Fruit shall develop and ripen and come to full growth.

The First Fruit is that of morality and purity of thought. This makes one a decent person who is able to progress on the Spiritual Path.

Secondly, there is security of position, so that the Temple of the Soul, which, naturally, is the body, is not damaged by excessive poverty or suffering.

It should be stated that in some conditions one has to have poverty and suffering because of Karma, but as a general rule it is better that one is able to attain to the Middle Way—not too rich, not too poor, not starving, but not overfed.

The Third Fruit is that by which one has one's legitimate desires fulfilled. It comes as a reward for right living, right thinking, right behaving.

A legitimate desire does not include the desire of having a new car or a new coat, or things which are for vanity or to show off to other people.

A legitimate desire is a desire to help others and to save others from unnecessary distress. It is also legitimate to desire to progress and advance, again unselfishly, again so that one may help others.

The Fourth, and best, of the Fruits is that one shall speedily attain to release from the ties of this world. It means liberation from Karma, the end of one's incarnations and reincarnations upon the Earth system. When one has the last of the Four Fruits, when one has escaped from the toils of the Earth, then one can, if one is foolish, volunteer to come back to this dreary old spot to help others. When you attain to that position, and you are on the 'Other Side,' leave instructions that if you ever decide to volunteer your friends will have your sanity tested, because it does appear that nowadays things are rather out of hand on the Earth, and things are much too hard. However, we are in the Age of Kali, and that gloomy Age will pass away and the Sun will shine again with the dawn of a new era, and with an upsurge of spiritual purity.

G

GAYATRI: This is the name given to a most important Mantra. Christians recite The Lord's Prayer, which, after all, is just a Christian Mantra. The Hindu recites the Gayatri.

A Hindu will go through certain ceremonies, and then recite this Mantra daily. Here are the actual words: 'Om, bhur, bhuvah, swah. Tat savitur varenyam bhargo devasya dhimahi. Dhiyo yo nah prachodayat. Om.'

The meaning of this translated into English is: 'We meditate upon the ineffable effulgence of that resplendent Sun. May that Sun direct our understanding for the good of all living.'

This is a Mantra which could be recited by Christians with much profit!

GHOST: That eerie thing which swishes around in the night with a few creaks and groans, and which causes the hair on our heads to stand straight up, is harmless!

A ghost is just an etheric force which wanders about according to the habits of its previous owner, until eventually that etheric force, that etheric double, is dissipated. A strong healthy person who is suddenly killed by perhaps extreme violence, has a very strong etheric. If a person is being attacked, then he or she focuses the etheric into a strong entity. If, then, the Silver Cord is suddenly severed in that process which we call death, the astral body goes off, the physical body decays, and the poor etheric becomes a homeless, mindless, wandering waif. Throughout the whole life of the body, the etheric has been modelled on that body, it is a habit pattern of the body. So if the body was in the habit of going to a certain place, or thinking of certain people, then the etheric will do likewise until perhaps during centuries the power becomes dissipated, and eventually vanishes.

The etheric body is the one which attends seances and gives the so-called 'messages' from beyond the grave. It is quite a tragedy really because people on Earth should realise that when we leave this world we have other things to do, and cannot always, and do not want always, to get in touch with people left behind. The etheric, or ghost, is a thing of no moment and should be disregarded.

Supposing you were in some city and very busy with some special task requiring concentration, would you like it if some person kept phoning you from some other city, kept phoning you and asking you all sorts of stupid questions? You would soon get tired of the whole thing. In the same way, the real entities, whom, if you like, you can call Souls, do not like being disturbed, they have too much else to do.

GIVE: There is an old occult law which states, 'Give that you may receive.' If you do not give you cannot receive. If you are too mean to give anything, or too selfish, then you lock a shell around yourself so you cannot receive even if a would-be giver is most anxious to give.

In the Christian belief it is stated that as you sow so shall you reap. It is also stated 'Cast your bread upon the waters.' And yet again, 'It is more blessed to give than to receive.'

46

It is utterly, utterly essential that if you want to receive something, then you have to give something. Not necessarily money, you may have to give of yourself, that is, give love, give friendship, give attention, sympathy, give help, understanding. It is useless to say, 'What is mine is mine, and what is yours I want too.' Unless you are prepared to GIVE you cannot possibly receive. So, those of you who button up your wallets or make sure that your purse-strings are drawn up tight, remember that if you are going on your knees to start praying it is a waste of your time as well of everyone else's, it is useless to pray for things unless you are willing to give things.

GOD: According to the Raja Yoga there is no concept of a God. The Vedantas and The Bhagavad Gita state definitely that the Yogi reaching liberation from the body finds himself as a God.

For those who want to look it up, the term for God is Ishwara. Vedantic teaching is that all mankind is a part of God, and there are four main stages of approaching Godhood:

1. Nearness to God.
2. Similiarity to the teaching of God.
3. Associating with a Godlike Being.
4. Living with a God.

According to the Christian belief, how many Gods do you think there are? Have you read Genesis? If not, read where God said, 'Let there be firmaments.' In other words, God is commanding a second God to make the firmament, and the second God obeyed and made the firmament. Then the first God said, 'Let there be light,' and the second God made light—not electric light or gas light or daylight, of course, but spiritual light, the light which gleams at the end of our own long, long trail of the upward Path of Evolution.

By the way, it is also worth remembering that many people read the Bible incorrectly. Most people believe that Adam was the first man created, but that is not correct. Read Genesis 4, 16 and 17; that shows Cain going forth into the land of Moab, and buying a wife. Now, if Adam was the first man created how was it possible for Cain to go and buy a wife? There must have been another man connected with it all somewhere else. One should remember that many of the teachings of the Bible were written for a people who were not educated, not really able to think for themselves, thus the Bible was written in simple language, often in parable form.

GRANTHIS: This peculiar word means a form of knot. There are three 'knots,' the basal, the heart, and the eyebrow knot.

In time everyone has to raise the Kundalini in order to progress spiritually and metaphysically. Raising the Kundalini means that one has to break through these knots, it means that one has to break free from physical lusts, free from physical desires and spites. When one has gone through the first of the knots, then one has to break through the ordinary higher mental desires; one has to do away with mental snobbery, for instance. Even some of the higher mental thoughts are concerned with selfishness, and before one can progress one has to truly remember that 'Race, creed, and colour do not matter, for all men bleed red.' And all men are equal in the sight of God.

The third knot on the spiritual plane is breaking through to one's own real self, the Overself, and then one is far beyond the confines of the physical body. When one breaks the third knot one does not need to come to this Earth, except specifically to help others.

It is worth commenting at this stage that so long as people think of will, will-power, and reason, then one is bound to the physical body just as is a person who always thinks of physical love and forgets that the real love is on the spiritual plane.

Many people have asked about love on the spiritual plane; it is a pure love, an absolute love, and nothing can approach the feeling of being with one's own 'twin soul,' because, although it is a horrible sounding term—'twin soul'—it is a very real thing indeed, and when one has one's twin soul in the Overself stage, then one is never forced back into incarnation but only comes back to help others.

GUNAS: There are three qualities which we simply must have. We must enter, progress through, and discard, passing ever higher and higher.

First there is sluggishness and neglect. From neglect one experiences pain such as hunger or cold. From the pain or neglect effort results in order that there may be relief from hunger or pain. This effort produces pleasure, the pleasure of eating in order that hunger may be appeased.

From the introduction to pleasure which comes when hunger is appeased, there arises a desire for pleasure, and thus a definite seeking for pleasure, causing energetic action which forms a habit, and the habit of restlessness.

From the excessive habit of seeking after pleasure, and obtaining pleasure, pain and neglect arises and the body suffers therefrom. From seeking too much pleasure we eat too much, and we get a pain where we should not. This pain causes us to think—which in itself is quite a feat! We think along the causes of our pain, and then we decide not to do that which caused the pain, and sometimes we actually do refrain from doing harmful things. Most people do it 'just once more,' but until they can cut out their 'just once's' no progress can be made. Progress can only be made when we eat to live and do not live to eat.

GURU: That wondrous, misunderstood word merely means 'A weighty person.'

A Guru means in its commonly accepted term, One whose words are worthy of consideration. A Guru is a Teacher, a spiritual Teacher, and he should be an illumined soul, one who has raised the Kundalini and knows how to raise it in others.

When the student is ready the Master will appear. The student cannot and should not and must not exclaim, as so many do, 'Show me the Great Masters, let them come to me and I shall believe.' The Adepts who have remarkable powers of perception, whose faculties have been sharpened and purified, are not able to teach those who just bleat feebly that they, and they alone, are worthy of Great Teachers. Those immature, unevolved people who demand that a Teacher accepts him or her as a pupil—well, they delay their own progress.

It is worth a comment here to show what happens: I had a letter some time ago from England, some idiot wrote in a most condescending manner stating that, 'Mr. So-and-So is prepared to accept Lobsang Rampa as his Teacher if Lobsang Rampa will give immediate proof that he can do all that he says.' The attitude of Lobsang Rampa, and many others, is to toss such letters in the waste-paper basket with a sigh of regret at the folly of those who write thus.

A true Guru, according to the full meaning of the word, is as rare as a horse with feathers, because the true Guru must be more or less sinless, must be more or less without feelings of self, and must have no desire for fame. The poor fellow must, in fact, exist almost without being. It is permitted, of course, that the Guru has enough to live upon and enough to see that he is decently clad.

Remember, remember, remember, 'When the student is ready the Master will appear.' The student, being untrained (otherwise he would not be a student!) is never, never, never in a position to say that he is ready to be taught. That is the surest way of saying that he is not.

GURUBHAI: This refers to any male person studying under the same spiritual Teacher. One should also give the name applying to a female because nowadays the ladies, the so-called weaker sex, are often the stronger sex when it comes to spirituality. So, ladies, if you study under the same spiritual Teacher you are a Gurubhagini.

Gurus are often referred to as 'Master.' That is completely and absolutely and utterly wrong. A Guru is a Guru, 'a weighty counsellor,' not a Master. A Master implies that one is forced to do what the Master says; a Guru advises and leaves the student full choice of action. So, please, never Master: Guru, counsellor, adviser, teacher, or anything similar, but why not stick to—Guru?

H

HABIT: A habit is that action, or series of actions, which have become impressed upon our subconscious so that we may perform even intricate operations or manoeuvres without conscious effort or the intervention of the conscious mind.

The life and actions of most people is merely the following of habits. Most people could just as well be automatons; they get up at the same time in the morning because of habit, they do things at the same time of day because of habit. People smoke—even knowing that it is killing them!—because of habit.

Habit starts like the gossamer thread of a spider's web. One thread is weak and can easily be broken, but lay those threads side by side so that you have a hundred, a thousand, a million threads, and one would be immovably bound, powerless, almost impotent to break the habit without really determined efforts.

Look upon habit as upon a series of binding threads. Replace bad habits with good habits. That will make it like replacing each thread individually instead of trying to snap the whole. You cannot take away a thing without replacing it with something more suitable.

If you are a pessimist, smile instead of scowl, it is easier to smile. Make a habit of smiling, make a habit of being kind to people, make a habit of being honourable and keeping your word. Soon you will be a different person, a person whom all will admire and respect. Habit is one of the most important things of life, and a good habit helps one, but a bad habit stultifies one's development.

HALASANA: This is sometimes referred to as the Plough Posture. It should be emphasised again that all these exercises really do not do anyone any good. Sometimes it is claimed that it develops spiritual discipline, but if one already has the discipline necessary to tie oneself in a knot, then surely that discipline can be directed into far more useful channels.

Let me put on record that I regard all these 'exercises' as crackpot inventions designed to lead one away from true progress. But if you want to try the Plough Posture, here it is:

Lie on your back, keep your arms parallel and very tightly pressed against your body. Press your palms against the floor. Take a deep breath (you will need it!), and then raise your legs and move them up and over your body so that your legs are over your head and your toes are touching the ground beyond the top of your head.

Raise up your body as much as possible, and put your arms around your head. This particular exercise makes one assume the shape of an old-fashioned plough.

If you want to do shapes, etc., etc., it is much more comfortable to have a darkened room and a white wall, and put your hands between a lighted candle and the wall, then you can make all sorts of shapes in shadow, rabbits and cats and things like that. It's much more fun and much more comfortable.

HARI: Sometimes people call Vishnu by that name, but actually Hari means 'to take away.'

The mistake arose in an original translation because Vishnu was alleged to remove sins and faults by love and wisdom. Actually, of course, we can only remove faults and sins ourselves by adopting the right attitude to life, and towards others.

There are other meanings attached to Hari.

HARI BOL: This means 'chant the name of the Lord that ye may be purified and your sins may be washed away.'

HARI OM: This meaning of Hari is that of a sacred syllable, or actually, to be strictly correct, sacred syllables.

By repeating 'Hari Om, Hari Om, Hari Om' when one is alone, of course, one's own personal vibrations may be increased, one's spirit may be elevated, and so one approaches more closely to one's God.

Friendly advice—if you try any of these syllables or exercises, then do it when you are alone or people will look at you suspiciously and send for the man in the white coat which ties at the back !

HARMONY : There are stated to be Three Powers of Divinity. Harmony is one of those Powers.

It is necessary to have all organs of the human body in harmony with all other organs in the body. If you have that, then the result is a person who is well balanced and healthy.

A person with harmony in the mind is one who has pure love and compassion for others, and that person is able to assist others without thought of self-gain.

If all people of this world had harmony within them this would indeed be the Golden Age, because then there would be no difficulty in following the Rule which says, 'Do as you would be done by.'

HATHA-YOGA : This is just a series of exercises, a system of physical exertion. It is meant to give one mental or spiritual discipline, or something like that, but it is concerned only with postures of the body and need not be taken in any way seriously. It should be borne in mind that the true Masters of the Occult, the true Adepts, never go in for this Hatha-Yoga stuff.

According to the people who do try these stunts, 'Ha' means the sound of a breath going in, and 'Tha' is the sound of the breath coming out.

The really evolved person does not go in for these circus turns without, of course, being in a circus, and these rather stupid exercises merely take one's attention from that which is more essential—spirituality and the desire to help others.

The practitioners of these exercises have a wholly inflated idea of their own importance, but that only means that spiritually they are very poorly evolved.

There ARE systems of Yoga devoted to the attainment of spiritual perfection, of course, but Hatha-Yoga is not one of them.

HEAD : Apart from being that knob which protrudes from the end of the neck and bears the organs of sight, sound, and smell, the head also contains the mechanism through which one can receive messages from the Overself, and transmit messages to the Overself.

The head is a rather delicate contraption which suffers from the fact that all blood supplies, all nervous energies, must go through a rather narrow channel in the already narrow neck. It follows that the head should be well balanced so that there is no undue constriction of the spinal cord.

A very good exercise to get balance of the head is to put two or three heavy books on the head, and provided that you can keep them there long enough, put your hands on your hips out of the way, and then walk up and down the room several times without shedding the books in the process.

This is not to be confused with any Hatha-Yoga 'exercise,' but this is a definite thing to enable one to attain poise. It will help your poise, and will also help your posture. It will cause you some pleasurable surprise, too, that you can walk up and down with a load of books on your head.

If you want to do things properly, have a basin of ice-cold water on your head, because then you have an incentive to do it seriously.

In the East the small boys who are going to be monks of any kind sometimes have a bowl full of hot wax in which there is a lighted floating wick. The wretched boy walks up and down the corridors with this bowl on his head. If he cannot balance, and the bowl spills, the hot wax goes on his clothes and he spends the next day scrubbing them clean.

Only small boys, and possibly small girls, do these things. The person who has progressed, even a little, does not have to indulge in such things.

HEALING: When we refer to healing we do not intend to indicate the stuff dispensed by the local doctor. Our reference to 'healing' is that process carried on by the etheric double during the physical sleep of the material body.

The material body gets a lot of misuse and abuse during the day, so when the astral body is out wandering during the night the etheric double carries out the work of the repair man, or repair woman, whichever the case may be.

Certain people have healing power which means that they possess a super-abundance of etheric energy which they can pass to another person with a deficiency. Thus it works in much the same way as a blood transfusion, only in this case

53

one transfuses energy and the will-power which is necessary to make a sick person decide to recover.

HIGHER SELF: This is our Overself, the piece of us which controls the physical body from afar. We, down here on Earth are 'pulling the chestnuts out of the fire for our Overself.' I does not matter unduly if we get our fingers burnt, because ou fingers have to last a few years only, but the Overself has to las throughout Eternity and a bit longer.

We can feed the spirit part of us by meditation, by contemplation, and by seeing the good which we have learnt through the incarnate experiences.

We have to develop love and good sense. We must develop and practise understanding. We must avoid doing those things which cause pain and distress to others, for although while on this world it is easy to delude other people, to lead them astray, and although possibly we are so clever that we are immune to the laws of the Earth, yet when we once pass beyond the confines of this Earth we find that we have to pay for all the misery we have caused others, we have to pay for all the losses which we have inflicted upon others. Thus it is, in commonsense terms, cheaper for us to behave ourselves while on this Earth, because this is just a blink of the eye compared to the Greater Life beyond.

HSIN: This is a Chinese word meaning 'Good Faith,' meaning that we must act so that those around us have respect for us, and so that our behaviour enhances instead of detracts from the stature of the human race.

HSUAN HSUEH: This is a very deep metaphysical concept and doctrine which started in the third century in China. It is a doctrine of mystical experiences which in some ways resemble the Egyptian mysteries, but it is not often practised now because of the long, long years of study necessary.

Of course, when one is able to do astral travelling consciously, once can go in the astral and learn there in the matter of minutes all those things which takes the Hsuan Hsueh student a lifetime.

One of the ordeals which those students had to undergo was this; before a student could pass into a higher grade he was *killed,* and the astral allowed to go free. By special methods the blood was maintained in the brain so that no brain damage occurred. But the student had great experiences in the astral, and was then revivified.

The awakened student was never the same after! Knowing what was the other side of life, he was more careful of his own actions, particularly how his actions affected the lives of others. HYPNOTISM : Most people do not realise the terrible force latent in hypnotism. Hypnotism should never, never, never be used except under the most stringent conditions.

Any person, unless he has been specially trained, can be hypnotised. It does not matter if the person is extroverted or introverted; any person can be hypnotised.

Hypnotism is a state of heightened awareness. The person hypnotised is aware only of that person who has hypnotised him, he is unable to determine between right and wrong.

A person who is going to be hypnotised believes that he can be hypnotised. He may not believe it consciously, but subconsciously he believes he can be hypnotised, and so his state of tension actually helps to hypnotise him!

In hypnotism a form of disassociation occurs. The small part of the entity which is conscious of right and wrong is driven away—confined, restricted, removed from the scene of operations, leaving behind the nine-tenths of the sub-conscious.

The sub-conscious is like some blundering great lout who has no reason, who is not able to tell right from wrong, but somehow has obtained a lot of information and the power to move about.

With the censor, or one-tenth of the mind, out of action there are no limits to what the nine-tenths will do.

The person doing the hypnotising can persuade the subject—the one hypnotised—that the fully loaded revolver which the latter holds is just a toy water-pistol. Thus, if the hypnotiser convinces the hypnotised person's sub-conscious that it is all a joke to pull the trigger and squirt water, then the hypnotised subject will pull the trigger and kill the object of the attack.

It is a terrible thing to hypnotise a depressed person, and to assure that person that he or she is now happy, because it can make neurotic habits very much stronger, and it can bring about suicide.

The person who goes to parties and hypnotises just for the fun of it is a menace who should be removed to a padded cell because he can cause others to go to a padded cell!

Almost anyone can be hypnotised, and when a person has been hypnotised several times that person can be made to do *anything at all,* it is all a matter of suggesting the action in such a way that the hypnotised person believes that he or she is doing good. Then having been so persuaded the hypnotised person can be made to do anything whatsoever the hypnotiser desires. Statements to the contrary are designed merely to cover up the terrible danger which exists in hypnotism.

Hypnotism is actually a crime against the Overself, because it is a crime to tamper with the mechanism which the Overself controls. It can cause one to have a Karma which will take incarnation after incarnation to clear up. So if any of you have a desire to hypnotise, or to be hypnotised, think again, and then refrain.

In the hands of a genuine specialist—not a stage performer—hypnotism can be used successfully to probe past incarnations. A person, always in the presence of witnesses, of course, and with a tape-recorder running, can be progressively hypnotised and asked questions about different ages even before being born to this Earth. It takes a very, very great deal of experience before the hypnotist is safe to undertake such things.

AUTO-HYPNOTISM: This is a process under which a person is able to disassociate the conscious and the sub-conscious, and in which the conscious part of one acts as the hypnotising agent. Under certain conditions it is possible to correct bad habits of character and to strengthen good habits. But, again, one should not normally indulge in auto-hypnosis unless one has first had a thorough medical examination to make sure that one is sound physically, and—let me add—mentally. Hypnotism is a sword with three edges instead of only two or one, and it should be left well alone except by the accredited experts.

I

ICHCHHASHAKTI: This is the long way to say 'will-power.' Actually, it is not just the power which enables one to say, 'I can' and 'I will,' but is, instead, rather more like the electric waves generated by the brain, and which can, literally, galvanise one into a special form of activity.

It is the special power which enables the Adept, who is breathing correctly, to accomplish levitation. Levitation is quite possible, and rather easy to do, especially if one really has a sound reason for it.

This 'will-power' is that which enables us to see into the

future, or into the probable future, and which enables us within a limited extent to pre-order future occurrences. It is the power by which so-called 'coincidences' take place.

There is no actual Western term for this, but it is a special power of the will acting at the instigation of the Overself which enables the physical body and the astral body to co-operate to an unusual extent to produce certain effects.

IDA: This is a column of sensory and motory nerves on the left side of the spinal cord. These nerves, or bunches of fibres, have a special place in the relationship between the physical and astral bodies. The fibres coil around and end at the left nostril. By using certain breathing exercises one can cause palpation of the Ida, and so awaken certain dormant centres.

It is not proposed to give that special breathing exercise, although others are given at the end of this Dictionary. To give this particular exercise might be to cause harm to someone who read and rushed without knowing what it was all about. One has to remember that many people will go into a library, pick up a book, and just copy out a paragraph or two to save the price of a book, and to protect those people who are trying to run before they can walk such an exercise must be omitted.

IGNORANCE: Ignorance is lack of knowledge, lack of wisdom, and if we were not so foolishly ignorant we should not have so many troubles. The ignorant person does not know enough to know that he does not know. Perhaps the best way to explain it is:

He that knows not and knows not that he knows not, he is a fool, shun him.

He that knows not and knows that he knows not, he is teachable, teach him.

He that knows and knows that he knows, he is wise, follow him.

ILLUSION: This particular planet is called on other planes the World of Illusion, the world where one's senses deceive one, the world where things are very different from what they seem. People on 'the Other Side' think of those on the Earth as being afraid to go to Hell. Well, Earth is one of the hells, it is where we get the hell of physical experience and the hell of illusions.

We look upon this world which we call the Earth, and we think it is the most wonderful thing ever. We think the whole Universe and Universes beyond were made specially and exclusively for this Earth; we think we are the only creatures alive in space; we think that millions and billions, and trillions and trillions of other worlds are empty, desolate, just put up there as a peep-show for Mankind.

We think that we are Godlike creatures, the like of which has never been seen before and will never be seen again.

That is illusion. Earth is a speck of dust and no more. Earth is one of the smaller specks of dirt in the sky. We think, while we are on this Earth, that we are great and powerful, we think that our riches will buy the Kingdom of Heaven. But there is no bargain basement beyond this Earth. We cannot get salvation at cut rates, we have to get rid of illusion and get down to the true meaning of things. We have to get rid of selfishness and lust, we have to get rid of our callous disregard for the other person. Until we are ready to give of ourself we cannot receive of others. It is an illusion to think that we can.

IMAGINATION: Imagination is the picturing of one's desires or one's fears, and imagination is the greatest force of all, greater than will-power, greater than love. It is an old lore of psychologists that in any battle between the will and imagination, the imagination always wins, and if we try to conquer imagination by brute will-power then we cause a neurotic condition. The imagination still wins because the imagination causes a breakdown, so that the imagination must conquer.

There cannot be love without imagination. One imagines the charms of one's beloved, or one imagines that one has met one's 'twin soul' (as rare as apples on a gooseberry bush while on Earth!), and one imagines all the pleasures with love undying of being married to such-and-such a person. In passing, it needs rather more than just animal passion to keep two people in harmony.

If the imagination says that one shall not do such-and-such a thing, then, no matter how strong the will, a person cannot do it. Could you, for instance, walk along a plank suspended across the tops of two ten-story buildings? No matter how strongly the plank was anchored your over-worked imagination would say that you were going to fall, and then you would fall, to the delight of the onlookers and to the profit of the Press who would be sure to be there.

If you want to get results you will have to control your imagination so that it and friend will-power work together in harmony.

58

INCARNATION: Homo sapiens who so often lacks the latter, is just one method of enabling an Overself to gain experience. There are people on an enormous number of planets, as is now being recognised by reputable scientists all over the world. Some of them are trying to tune in on radio messages from other worlds, and even as long ago as the beginning of the century a very famous man, Nicholas Tesla, who was one of the inventors of the radio tube or valve (depending on whether you are in the U.S.A. or England), reported that he had received signals from another planet. Marconi reported the same, but these two eminent gentlemen were such objects of ridicule that they dropped research like a hot potato—a very hot potato. But now the U.S. Government and the U.S.S.R. Government are doing everything possible to initiate success. Possibly the Communists want to convert a few more planets to Communism.

People come to this Earth to gain experience of a special kind. According to some teachings, Earth is hell!

A person comes to Earth in order to have sharp experiences which can be analysed by the Overself, and which the Overself could not gain in such a short time. People come to Earth time after time working through every sign of the Zodiac, and working through each of the quadrants of the Zodiac, in much the same way as a student at a college takes various courses of instruction in order to get a balanced knowledge. Thus a person can become Aries in one life, and the opposite sign in the next life. In succeeding incarnations the poor soul can go through all the Houses or Signs of the Zodiac, and each quadrant of each Sign, and thus gain complete experience of all the unpleasant happenings which occur to humans.

When one has learned, and not had any great desire to come back to this Earth, then the person is rid of incarnations on this Earth plane. After, when one leaves as when one leaves school, one takes up the work for which one has been trained.

INDRIYAS: More correctly it should be 'The Ten Indriyas' because there are ten organs in the body by which the Overself can gain various specialised information.

There are the organs of perceptions, the organs of hearing, sight, smell, taste, and touch; and the organs of more direct action which are the organs of excretion, generation, propulsion (feet), touch (hands), and taste (tongue).

Each of these organs relays back through the spinal cord and up into the brain everything that is happening. The information is broadcast to the Overself, who thus is in touch with everything that is happening and becomes aware of every sensation. When this relay system breaks down we can see the results in a mental home when we look at catatonic patients.

INTUITION: A process under which the physical body is given a glimpse of something which normally in the physical body could not be known.

For example, a person can be standing on a sidewalk, and can then have a sudden flash of intuition that a chimney-pot or a slate is going to fall on his head. The man cannot see the chimney-pot, and cannot hear it either, but he usually looks up in time to see the thing before it hits him!

When people will believe in intuition, and give it rein to develop and blossom forth, it can be a very useful thing indeed. Actually, the Overself who is not yet ready to have the body damaged, can give a preliminary warning of a danger to come and thus to be avoided.

When one gets an impression that a person is near, when a person is perhaps within six or seven feet, it does not mean that that is intuition, it just means that either telepathy or impinging or auric emanations is taking place.

It is often stated that women have greater intuition than men, and if you will look at some of the illustrations in *You— Forever* you will observe that a woman's etheric and aura have a rather different shape to that of a man, and so it gives them greater intuition.

ISHVARAKOTI: This is an inferior type of Avatar. The person who comes to this Earth for the good of others, and who is normally free of the bonds of the Earth and thus has no Earth Karma, may be an Ishvarakoti. If he or she is dealing with individuals on a minor scale, then it will be an Ishvarakoti.

An Avatar is very much more evolved and does not necessarily come from this Universe at all, nor from the next or the one after that. An Avatar is one who teaches and restores to present-day requirements ancient teachings.

ISHWARA: Some people use this word as meaning, or indicating, God. This is particularly so among the Brahmans.

The actual meaning is 'Divine willer,' the Supreme Giver. It is a Perfect Being who has compassion for struggling humanity because the Being has worked through all the rounds of existence and knows how difficult it can be, and having suffered the Being has sympathy and understanding.

J

JAGRAT: This refers to the waking state, being awake in the body as opposed to being asleep in the body. Being in a condition where one is aware of that which is occurring about one, where one is able to see, to hear, to speak, to feel, etc.

People are aware during the daytime, they know what is going on about them, they are able to attend to their business, but most people are not aware during their sleep, and it is necessary to be so aware before one can consciously do astral travelling, because the physical body must have rest, but the astral does not require rest—not for a few thousand years anyway—and thus if the physical body is resting and the astral body is just held captive, or wandering unguided in the wilderness, there is much waste of opportunity.

JAPA: A word which means 'repetition.' It has nothing at all to do with meditation, but merely indicates that one repeats a word with the idea that perhaps one can get help from other sources. Sometimes they can!

In Tibet people used to go about mumbling, 'Om, Om, Om,' and sometimes twirling a prayer wheel. In India people will say, 'Ram, Ram, Ram,' when they are sore afraid or in need of spiritual consolation. Presumably in the latter case they hope that Rama, whom they often consider to be a God, will come rushing to their help.

In much the same way, in parts of Europe, people will call upon their own God time after time. That is Japa.

JATI: This is one's personal status in the physical world. How are you? Are you rich, poor, healthy, or ill? Jati refers solely to one's material status, and must not be confused with the spiritual standards. It must also be stated that sadly enough those who are richest in material things are frequently quite impoverished in spiritual matters.

JEN: This is a word from the Chinese. It means the art of being human, humanity. It means love and kindness towards one's fellow man. It means being charitable and having benevolent feelings towards one's fellow man.

Jen is the basis of the Teachings of Confucius.

JIVA: A name for the individual living unit, complete with body, mind, various senses, and all that which makes up one human being. Usually this unit, this human being, is not aware of its purpose here on Earth, and it experiences birth, pleasure, pain, death, and all that which makes up life on Earth.

Frequently it rails at the unkind fate which sent it down to Earth, 'Well, I didn't ask to be born, did I?' unknowing the reason and unprepared to learn that which has to be learned.

If people knew how simple it is to die, if they knew that no one is ever discarded, no one is ever fried eternally, then perhaps they would think 'Oh, I will have a good time in this life, I can easily come back and clear up the mess in the next life.' Thus, they have to 'drink of the Waters of Leith,' so that the memory of past lives is swept away because not until they have reached a certain stage can they know——

JNANA: This is knowledge, awareness of life beyond the life of the world. It is knowledge of the Overself, knowledge of why one comes to the Earth, what one has to learn, and how one has to learn it. It is the knowledge that although an Earth life may be a terrible, terrible experience, yet it is just the twinkling of an eye in the time of the Greater Life.

Poor consolation while we are down here!

JNANI: This is a person who knows, a person who follows the road of knowledge, one who tries to reach to the Greater Reality and to escape from the shackles and pains of life on Earth. A person who can approach this stage is indeed approaching liberation or Buddhahood.

K

KAIVALYA: Upon this Earth most people are unaware of what they were in a past life, unaware of why they have come back to this Earth. People say, 'Oh, we only have one life, let's make the most of it!' These are blind people, blind spiritually, blind mentally. When they have reached the state of Kaivalya they will be aware of what awaits them on the other side of that which is called Death.

That word, Kaivalya, means liberation from the blindness and the follies of the world.

KAMA: This is desire, a craving. It is a memory of the pleasures and the pains previously experienced. Often these memories are the causes of habits such as smoking or drinking.

A person smokes because of some pleasure imagined in connection with smoking, or because you have to be a smoker to be 'grown-up.' If people could only remember how sick they were the first time they smoked they wouldn't do it.

People who drink intoxicants, well, it's a great pity, it's a stupid idea, in fact, because intoxicants drive one's astral body out of one's physical, and I don't blame the astral for getting out of such a stench as that left by stale spirits.

KARMA: This is an old law by which many people of the Eastern world regulate their lives. It is a very good law provided it is used in a common-sense manner.

You go to a shop and you buy a lot of goods. If you are lucky you can have them 'on the bill,' but you have bought your goods and they have to be paid for some time, you do not get them free.

You go through life and life after life doing things of which, in the still small hours of the morning, you regret, things of which you are ashamed when you are alone and can think about it, you do things which can harm another person. Well, it's a pity because as you sow so shall you reap.

In the same way, one should do kindnesses to others, 'Throw your bread upon the waters and it shall return to you.' Unfortunately, when it returns it may be a bit soggy, but that's not the idea. Do good to others, the more good you do, the more good has to be done to you.

If you come to Earth and you have a miserable time it means that you are being paid back for giving other people a miserable time in another life, and when you get to that happy, happy stage that you are living your last life on Earth, then you certainly will have a miserable time because you have to clear up all debts. Just as when you are ready to move to another district you rush around to the butcher, the baker, and the candlestick-maker (or should do if you are honest), and you pay what you owe. If you are an optimist you try to collect money which is owing to you, but that is a different matter. The law of Karma states that—Do as you would be done by because you have to pay back good as well as bad.

It is my personal belief that too rigid an adherence to the law of incarnation and the law of Karma may have been responsible for the degeneration of India and China, because in India as well as in China, people used to sit beneath the trees and say, 'Ah! So what? I have plenty more lives in front of me, let me sit like Ferdinand the Bull and smell the flowers in this life.' So it led to slothfulness.

As for China—I have actually seen this; a man fell in a river and definitely was drowning. None of the Chinese were remotely interested; they were asked afterwards why they had done nothing to save the drowning man. Their answer was to the effect that if they had saved that man FROM HIS KARMA, they would have had his Karma to deal with as well as their own. So, too rigid an adherence makes for apparent callousness. One has to take the good old Buddhist Way—not too bad or the police get after you, and not too good (impossible on this Earth!) or you are too pure to stay here. The Middle Way in all things. KLESHA: Actually there are five Kleshas because these are the names of the five main things which cause people trouble, cause people to come back to Earth time after time until they haven't any more Kleshas.

Klesha number 1—ignorance. And from ignorance there is conceit. If one has ignorance and conceit one is not able to perceive the faults within one and so eliminate them.

Desire of the wrong sort is another of the things which has to be avoided. Do you covet those things which you should not covet? Then you'd better look out, it's holding up your progress.

Aversion is another definite trouble. Aversion makes it difficult for one to 'get on' with another person, it makes one the square peg in the round hole, or is it the round peg in the square hole? It doesn't matter which, one is as bad as the other. One has to adopt the Middle Way, and not fall in love too often, but not hate people for too long.

Possessiveness is the fifth trouble. We might call people stingy, misers, grab-alls, scrooges, they are a miserable crowd anyhow, and until a person gets rid of possessiveness that person is not able to acquire because, to repeat an old story, one cannot receive until one is ready to give.

The Kleshas are the things which one must eradicate before one can break free of the round of birth, living, dying, rebirth. KNOWLEDGE: Knowledge? Do I need to explain what knowledge is? I think I do! We have to have three things before we can have knowledge. First, we must have inference, we must become aware of something, because until we are aware of a thing we cannot perceive its presence or its existence.

Secondly, we must have reliable information because until we have reliable information to support that which we infer we are not even starting to obtain knowledge.

Thirdly, we must have a form of intuition so that we may understand that which lies behind the matter which we have inferred and about which we have obtained reliable information. We have to have this intuition so that we may understand different aspects of which we desire to know about.

KOAN: This is a word from Zen Buddhism. People of the West often cannot make any sense out of a Koan, because it is a peculiar statement which apparently is without any logic and which has no sense whatever. But the student has to meditate upon it and supply a suitable answer.

No easy answer is possible, but when an answer does come to one, then it is usually as sudden as a burst of thunder; the answer comes as a revelation.

As a mild, mild, mild example let me say this as a specimen of a Koan:

'The gramophone record and the gramophone needle can produce music; listen to the music of the record without the needle.'

It is like trying to compare the abstract with the concrete, or trying to discuss a three-dimensional matter with a person who lives in one dimension.

KOSHA: This is a covering or sheath. Sometimes it is termed a container. There are five Koshas described in certain Upanishads. These are located each within the other. The inner one is the body which is fed by food, that is, the physical body, and if you want the Eastern name for it, it is Annamayakosha.

The second is the body of Prana, and this is the part which keeps mind and body together. The Eastern name for it? Pranamayakosha.

Third, we have the sheath of the mind which has the sense impressions. This contains the higher and lower minds. The Eastern word is Manomayakosha.

Fourth is the sheath, or body, of intellect or wisdom. This is the start of the Buddhi, and the Eastern name for this fourth Kosha is Vijnanamayakosha.

The fifth Kosha is the body of bliss, and which often is referred to as the Ego. It is 'A Sheath of Joy,' and the Eastern name is Anandamayakosha.

KOWU: This is a Chinese word which means the study, or investigation, of occult matters, and the rectification of misunderstandings which have occurred in previous studies.

KRIYA YOGA: This is a branch of Yoga which has three sections. The first section enables one to control the body and the functions of the body.

The second section gives one the ability to study mental things and to develop the memory so that one is able to obtain from the sub-conscious all that which one has previously learned.

The third gives one a desire to be attentive to one's spiritual requirements. It gives one an incentive to put aside the things of the flesh, and to progress through spirituality rather than through one's bank balance.

By devoting oneself to Kriya one can subdue the Kleshas which are the bane of human life.

KUMBHAKA: This is a special form of breathing, a special method or pattern of breathing. It is the retention of the breath between breathing in and breathing out, and much benefit can be obtained from practising according to certain fixed rules.

At the end of this Dictionary there will be a section devoted to different breathing exercises, so it is hoped that you will manage to keep breathing until you have read the words which come between this and that later section.

KUNDALINI: This is a life force. It is THE life force of the body. Just as a car cannot run without having electricity to fire the mixture in the cylinders, so humans cannot live in the body without the life force of Kundalini.

In Eastern mythology the Kundalini is likened to the image of a serpent coiled up below the base of the spine. As this special force is released, or awakened, it surges up through the different Chakras and makes a person aware of esoteric things. It awakens clairvoyance, telepathy, and psychometry, and enables one to live between two worlds, moving from one to the other at will without inconvenience.

The Kundalini is a dangerous thing indeed, and one should not try to awaken that Kundalini without absolutely adequate supervision from an Adept. You cannot do it by reading a book! If you meddle about and awaken your Kundalini the wrong way it can lead to madness. It is one of the most dangerous things in this world to try to raise the Kundalini without knowing what you are doing.

The average human is only one-tenth conscious. Perhaps,

actually, that flatters the average human! The point is that if one can raise the Kundalini one becomes very much more conscious, one can dominate others. But when one has raised the Kundalini one loses the desire to dominate others for self-gain.

People wonder where exactly is the Kundalini, where is 'at the base of the spine?'

The Kundalini force actually starts midway between the organ of generation and the organ of excretion. Now, having given you that information it is suggested that you do not try experiments with the Kundalini unless you have a real Guru who can help you, and you must have utter faith in that Guru. If you have no Guru for the moment, remember—when the student is ready the Guru will appear, but the Guru knows, and the student does not know, when the student is ready.

The Bible story of Adam and Eve, complete with serpent and apple, is merely the story of Eve having her Kundalini awakened.

'The Serpent tempted Eve,' and Eve suggested naughty, naughty things to Adam who certainly learned fast, and took a hearty bite of the Apple of Knowledge. Now look at what happened to all us poor humans since!

Do you get it? Eve, the Mother of all Living, the same as now Mary is a more or less general term for Woman throughout the world. The serpent is the serpent force of the Kundalini, and the apple is the Fruit of Knowledge. So you don't meddle with the Kundalini, or it will bite your brains.

KUTHASTHA: This is the self, the true Overself, that part of one which stands above all the changing items of the world.

This is the part of one which enables one to feel friendship for those who would do one ill.

You can imagine that this Kuthastha is the one who stands above and looks down and supervises your actions; you can regard it as the Guardian Angel which is always watching to see what you are doing.

Kuthastha is that which stands beyond all illusions, that which cannot be deceived or misled. It is what you have to become eventually.

L

LAMP: To the Easterner a lamp is very similar to a life. A lamp is lit, the flame flickers for a brief period, then when the fuel is exhausted the flame subsides and dies, and there is perhaps a slight trail of smoke from the still-smouldering wick.

A lamp is often used in Eastern Teachings to symbolise the flame of life, to symbolise the impermanence of existence on Earth, and to symbolise also that we, by that life on Earth, should bring a little illumination to others around us.

An advanced Easterner is often likened to a lamp standing in a draught-free atmosphere where there are no turbulent currents of air to make the flame flicker.

It is also frequently stated in the Far East that it is better to light a candle than to curse the darkness, meaning that even the little flicker of a candle is better than no light. So every one of us, no matter how new we are upon the Path of Spirituality, can contribute something towards the evolution of mankind by showing the light of our spirituality, so that those who attempt to follow our own examples may find their footsteps so guided by the illumination which our own conduct, and our own spirituality, can provide.

It is worth remembering that the so-called suicide gestures of the Buddhist monks who drench themselves in petrol and then ignite the fumes, are again obeying an old Buddhist dictum which is to the effect that it is better to extinguish the flame of life than to have the flame of the spirit sullied and debased. So the Buddhist monk or nun who burns to death as a human lamp believes that in so doing he or she is making a noble gesture of protest against evil tamperings with the rights of mankind to believe as one will and to worship as one will.

In writing my books, which are true books—all that I have written is true and is my own personal experience, but that is by the way—let me repeat that in writing my books, particularly in writing *You—Forever* and this book, I am using as my motto 'I light a candle' in the hope that even this feeble flicker may prove a help and guide to those who know not which way to turn.

LAW: This is most frequently referred to as the Noble Eightfold Path. It is a complete code of living, a set of rules whereby people can live according to the Golden Rule of do as you would be done by. By following 'The Law' one can attain to a Buddhist state in much the same way as a Christian, following the Ten Commandments, can progress spiritually.

Naturally, as well as the Noble Eightfold Path, or 'The Law' which refers to it, there are other laws, the laws of nature, the laws of life itself. These cannot be disregarded, because the laws of nature determine what sort of body a man or a woman shall have, and the laws of life tell one that one has to follow certain rules that the physical body may continue until its task upon this Earth is accomplished.

It is a fact that all laws of Man are made for Man. Laws are made to govern the multitude, the mass of people who otherwise have no yardstick, no guidance, and have not yet attained to the position where they can live according to higher laws. One must remember that when one is dealing with an Avatar one here deals with a person who is not subject to the laws of the world, because he has progressed so that he can follow instead the laws of the universe, or of the universe beyond.

LAYA: The Kundalini, which as we have seen, is also called The Serpent Force, lies below the base of the spine ready to be raised, and to enable a person to flower into awareness of psychic matters.

Laya Yoga is a system of Yoga which specialises in 'the raising of the Kundalini.' Various tantras and mantras are used in order to increase the physical vibrations, and thus to—as it were—give the sleeping Kundalini a hearty shake in order that it may be awakened.

Again, please consider this warning that one should not try to raise the Kundalini without absolute awareness of what one is doing. Raising the Kundalini without proper supervision can lead to insanity, it can lead to dreadful things happening inside the mind, it can lead one straight into a mental home; but it is even worse than that, because one can do appalling things before being taken to the mental home.

To raise the Kundalini is to raise one's I.Q. This is because, at the present stage of evolution, Man is nine-tenths subconscious and only one-tenth conscious, so in raising the Kundalini one can be a few more tenths conscious, and it is like putting a small boy at the controls of the latest supersonic jet bomber which is all ready loaded and ready to take off.

As one who knows, as one who has seen much, suffered

much, and learned much, please carefully consider my warning: Do not try to raise the Kundalini until you know precisely what you are doing, and until you have a competent, pure-minded Guru beside you who is willing to supervise and protect you from your newly awakened self. People have quite a lot of bad in them still, and if the wrong part of one gets hold of the Kundalini then trouble is caused.

LEVITATION: Levitation is a very real thing indeed, it is not something out of Science Fantasy or Science Fiction or whatever you like to call it; it is not the pipe-dream of a person who has had too much alcohol! People who have never seen an airship of the gas-balloon type would be unable to believe that such a vast structure could rise into the air and move about. Consider, for instance, the impression upon people who have never seen an airship, who have never heard of air travel, if they were suddenly to see a zeppelin or one of the Goodyear blimps sailing across the sky, and perhaps throwing down a few bags of sand as ballast. They would not believe their own senses. Yet this is not so simple as levitation.

Many tribes in Africa were unable to believe that metal ships could float upon water. The obvious thing to them was that a piece of metal would sink in water, and so people of the interior could not believe in metal ships until they actually saw them.

We 'enlightened beings' know how gas balloons work, we know how heavy metal ships can float, and so we can smile superciliously at the ignorant natives who ran in fright.

Levitation is accomplished by a very special form of breathing which actually raises the frequency of the body's molecular oscillations, so that it is able to induce a form of contra-gravity. If one is expert enough, one can control the height at which one floats. If one is not so expert—well, it is to be hoped that they said goodbye to their friends and relations before practising.

In the East, in the great lamaseries and temples where such things are taught, all practices are first conducted indoors, so that the worst that can befall a novice is that he gets thumped on the head by the ceiling, and that often serves to teach him to study more assiduously.

Levitation cannot be done while there are scoffers gaping at one, because it demands concentration and a special form of breathing. Anyway, why should one go by levitation without one's luggage when you can go by a suitable airline and have a pretty, or not so pretty, air hostess (depending upon one's age and sex!) hold one's hand when one feels nervous?

Certain lamas, before the Communist invasion of Tibet, were able to cover long distances at fantastic speed. This is because they were able to do a minor form of levitation so that, their weight becoming appreciably less, they could leap perhaps fifty feet at one go. Thus, they progressed in fifty or a hundred-foot strides.

Under certain conditions a lama who is desperately ill can use a modified form of levitation to get himself off the ground in order that he may cope with an emergency. Of course he has to pay for it after, but the energy can then be paid back in small instalments over a week or so.

LI: This is a Chinese word which has two meanings.

Li in one sense means ritual, or standard of conduct—the ceremonies that one uses in order to get one into the right frame of mind to help with one's religious beliefs.

It can also mean rule of conduct, doing that which has to be done, and not doing that (no matter how enjoyable!) which should not be done.

The second meaning of Li is connected with the reason and that which is sometimes known in the Western world as 'The Eternal Verities.' This, of course, is just a highbrow way of saying the Great Truth, the Eternal Truths, which we all have to learn before we can progress to higher things, in much the same way as we have to learn the rules of the road before we can get a driving licence and drive a car.

There is, curiously enough, a third set of meanings for Li which is quite the opposite of good living, quite the opposite of righteousness. It deals, instead, with selfish gain.

Li is included in this Dictionary because you will come across the word if you are studying occult matters seriously. As an example, Li Hsueh Chia is a special form of study of Li. Easterners with Western tendencies call it Neo-Confucianism. Unless you are going into occultism thoroughly and to cover a diverse field, you can forget about this word.

LIBERATION: The Eastern term is Moksha, so it will be better to refer to that term, Moksha, for the meaning of liberation.

LILA: Some sects of Eastern belief are of the opinion that God, a great Being whom no one can fully visualise nor comprehend, created the world and all other worlds, and all that

71

are within those worlds, as a plaything, and parts of God entered into the puppets who were the humans, the animals, the trees, and the minerals. So the essence of God thus could live as all living creatures, gaining experience from the experience of all creatures.

Under this belief God sometimes needs another person to see what is happening to some of His faulty puppets, some of His little animals, some of His little humans, and let us not forget that humans are still animals.

God, wanting another person to see what is happening, would call upon yet another special person, an Avatar. Often a person cannot see the wood for the trees, and it is well known that the onlooker sees most of the game because the player is too busy. So the Avatar comes as an onlooker to see what it is that the player finds difficulty in seeing.

You will find more about the Avatar under the letter A.

Lila also means that which is relative, that which consists of time, space, etc. In other words, that which deals more with the abstract than it does with the concrete.

LINGA: Actually this is a sign representing Shiva, but it is also used to indicate a phallic symbol.

In the days of long ago the peoples of the Earth had the most interesting task of populating the Earth as quickly as they could. Hence it is that the priests, who thought that the more subjects they had the more power they would have, made an order and called it a Divine Order. The order was to the effect that everyone should be fruitful and multiply. People had great hordes of children because that strengthened individual tribes, and the bigger the tribe, the more powerful it became. So, under the 'Divine Instruction' of the priests the warriors of the big tribes invaded small tribes and killed off the men and captured the women so that these women could be used for making more little tribesmen, who then could go out and capture more and more small tribes. This is also called civilisation.

The male organ, or a representation of it, thus became an object of great worship, and in various parts of the world today such stone pillars are regarded with awe and veneration. It is an amusing fact that the cupolas and minarets of mosques and temples, and the spires of Christian churches, were of phallic-symbol origin.

In Ireland, a very, very old land indeed, there are what are called 'the round towers.' These towers, cylindrical, and sometimes taller than a church tower, had a rounded top. They were phallic symbols, symbols of fertility, symbols that one must not forget that the more numerous a nation the stronger it became, and the more easily it could conquer lesser nations.

As the Irish became converted to Christianity they found a fresh use for their phallic-symbol round towers; they used to climb up a special staircase inside the tower and peer out from the top so that they could see if invaders were coming to steal things from their lands or to capture people to use as slaves. The round towers were very useful for keeping watch for the predatory English, who looked upon hunting the Irish as almost a national sport. Naturally enough, the Irish looked upon such 'sport' with considerable disfavour.

While on the subject it might be worth mentioning that in addition to the phallic symbol of the male organ there are also phallic symbols of the female organ. In the East windows, doors, etc., are in the shape of the female organ!

LOKA: A Loka is a plane of existence, a plane which is a complete world to one who is there. We, upon this Earth, are solid creatures to each other. 'Ghosts' are solid creatures to other 'ghosts.' Everything is solid and substantial to creatures, or beings, or entities who are going to exist in that particular world or plane of existence.

There are various Lokas, various planes of existence. It would take too long to discuss them all, but, purely by way of illustration, let us remember there is the physical world of the Earth, and that world which is invisible to us while we are upon the Earth, but which becomes solid to us when we go into 'the astral.

When we are in the astral it is a solid, material world to us. And then the plane above becomes to us as the astral world was to us when we were in the physical world of this Earth. The higher we travel, the greater the rate of vibration of our physical and spiritual molecules.

A Master can see any of the Lokas up to his own station in evolution as plainly as he can see things upon the Earth. You will all find that when you polish up your halos and leave this Earth you will go to the third of the Lokas, where you will find that people are not so treacherous, not so vicious, and not so irresponsible as they are upon this Earth, which is one of the lower hells.

73

LOTUS: The Lotus symbolises many things to the Easterner. It is a sacred symbol of Far Eastern religion in much the same way as a crucifix is a symbol to a Christian.

The Lotus is a plant which grows on the dirtiest and muddiest of water, it grows in the foulest surroundings, and yet no matter how foul those surroundings, the Lotus remains pure and unsullied and quite uncontaminated by that which is around it.

A Lotus leaf rests upon the water, but it does not become wet. The Lotus is not moistened at all by water, and that can be taken as a symbol of non-attachment with which we shall deal later.

The petals of the Lotus have a special significance, and the Easterner departs from actual physical resemblance in referring to a thousand-petalled Lotus, for instance. There is the Lotus of the Heart, and the thousand-petalled Lotus of the Brain, and if you progress in your studies and your spirituality you may find that one day a person will offer a blessing to your holy Lotus Feet. This does not mean that you have suddenly grown roots instead of the usual human appendages; it means, instead, that you have for some peculiar reason been elevated in the other person's estimation, and you now occupy the status of a Godlike Being.

If you survive this, and if you progress quite a bit more, you may find that you are of the Lotus Eyes, or the Lotus might be referred to some other part of your anatomy. Never mind, it is meant as a compliment.

The significance of the Lotus, then, is merely this: the Lotus is known as the perfect flower, with a perfect arrangement of petals and leaves. It is a plant which is part of, yet remote from, its surroundings. It remains clean and unsullied in conditions which would contaminate anything else. It is a symbol of purity which was available even to the most uneducated and the most under-privileged of the East.

LOVE: This is a most misunderstood word, as is sex. Sex and love, love and sex, they are mixed, they are muddled. They are abused and misconstrued by present-day people.

Love, actually, is harmony between two people, or between two creatures of any kind. It does not mean that they are sexually interested, it means that each vibrates on a frequency which is completely compatible wth the frequency of the loved person.

74

Love is unselfish. A person will do things for love which he would not do for any money.

It is, of course, dreadfully unromantic, but if people vibrate on the wrong frequency, then it causes dislike, apprehension, or even actual physical fear. But if one person could do a few more wobbles a second, or rather, if one person could have his molecules agitated to go a bit faster, then disharmony disappears, harmony takes over—love takes over.

LOWER MIND: The lower mind is that part of our person which absorbs knowledge and stores it. If we knew how, as certain Easterners do, we could recall everything that ever happened to us, even from BEFORE we were born.

Actually, it is quite easy if one knows how and if one has the patience to practise. People who can do this are stated to have 'total recall.'

Total recall can, as stated, be accomplished by practice, but one should not do it unless one has a clear conscience because if you have total recall you can recall all the unpleasantnesses as well as the pleasant times, and the unpleasant things frequently appear even worse when looking back upon them.

Total recall is within our sub-consciousness, and if there is good reason for it a competent hypnotist can hypnotise a person a few times and gradually take him or her farther back into the dimmest recesses of the sub-conscious memory. It can be used for discovering why a person has certain inhibitions or fears.

It can be used, also, for deciphering old documents in a language which one does not understand, because if one is taken back through the space and time of one's sub-conscious one can even tap the racial memory of mankind. But, of course, a much easier system is to do correct astral travelling and then see the Akashic Record.

M

MACROCOSM: This is a word which indicates the larger world, the world which is beyond the limitation of the fleshly things of this sphere which we term 'Earth.'

While we are in our body, we are in the 'little world' or, a technical term—'Microcosm.' The 'micro' part indicates small, just as 'macro' indicates large.

While we are in this world we are upon a very small world, our whole existence is a very small thing, we are denizens of the Microcosm. We are much like dirty little grubs, or caterpillars which later become butterflies. A caterpillar is confined to the ground, and to stalks and leaves, but as a butterfly it can soar upwards into new dimensions. So it is that we, when we leave this minute form of life in which we are now existing, enter the Macrocosm.

MAGIC: Magic is merely the distortion of misunderstood scientific facts, or facts which the scientist in his blindness is not able to understand.

To the savage, flying a plane is magic. To the hardly less savage Westerner, levitation is magic. That which is impossible today because 'science' cannot explain it with certain stereotyped facts, is magic. When science belatedly catches up with magic, then magic ceases to exist and becomes 'scientific fact.'

Curare was once the magic of savage witch-doctors. Science said that it was all wishful thinking, but when the more Westernised form of witch-doctor, who called himself a scientist, investigated the matter he 'discovered' curare in his chemical laboratory, and thus it became a more respectable thing.

Do not be misled by 'magic.' It is merely the things which certain talented people can do today which the bumbling scientist may not be able to do for a hundred years.

MANAS: This is the thought power of a human. Human beings have certain power in the same way as a storage battery has power. If a person does not know how to use the power of a storage battery, then that power might just as well not exist. But if one knows how to connect wires to a storage battery, then one can do quite a lot of interesting things with it, or with the power from it. The same applies with a human; when one is able at will to tap the power of thought in a human, one can do quite a lot of normally difficult things. When a person is suitably trained he can do telepathy, clairvoyance, psycometry, astral travelling, etc.

At present the average person is in the position of a car which controls the driver, instead of, as it should be, the driver controlling the car. A human who is not able to control his thought-power is a human who is blinded, maimed, and not really living!

Think of a dictator whipping up the mass-hysteria of a

crowd, and moulding that crowd to do as he wishes. Think of the mass-hysteria of a football crowd. They all have their mind on one thing, and if some little matter happens to trigger their mind reactions, then one can have a very ugly incident.

When there is any large crowd of people thinking upon a common subject each person magnifies the thought-power of the other, and so the thought-power grows as a snowball grows when rolled downhill. Dictators know this; they plant excitable or hysterical people in a crowd, and the crowd, taking their cue from the hysterics, soon get in a frenzy of enthusiasm, rage, or anything that the dictator wants.

Manas can act something like telepathy, it can induce mass-hysteria, and it can make a whole crowd think and act as one.
MANIPURAKA: This is one of the Chakrams. This one is that which is at the level of the umbilicus or navel. It is the third of the seven common Yogic centres of consciousness, and in esoteric terminology it is referred to as The Wheel, or Lotus. It is so called because to a clairvoyant, or to one who can see the astral, 'petals' flap around by the umbilicus, and depending upon how one is thinking it can be termed a wheel with the spokes rotating, or as the Lotus undulating in the etheric wind.

A person who is of good intentions, and who is fairly pure, will have the petals of the Lotus or the spokes of the Wheel, whichever you prefer to call it, of a green colour. That indicates that the person is able and willing to learn and to assist others as much as possible.

As the person rises higher and higher in the scale of evolution the petals become more and more yellow, showing increasing spirituality and devotion.
MANTRA: Actually a Mantra is a particular name for God, but by common usage it now is taken to mean something else; it is a form of prayer, it is the repetition of something sacred whereby one gains power. If one repeats a Mantra conscientiously and reverently one attains to purification of thought.

A Mantra should only be used for good, and never for bad, for there is an old saying that 'He who digs a grave for another may fall in it.' Thus it is that Mantras should only be used for good, they should only be used unselfishly and to help others.

In the Christian Bible it is stated that faith moves mountains; the same could be said about a Mantra. A Mantra used properly has very, very strong effects, and the more it is used the more it builds up power. Here is a very simple illustration of how it builds up power:

A violinist can play a certain note on a violin. If he just touches on the note he only makes a sound, but if he keeps on at the same note he can cause a glass to shatter and crumble because playing on that note has induced a vibration in the glass which eventually becomes more than the elasticity of the glass can handle, and so the glass breaks. In the same way a Mantra increases the vibration for good or for bad, but when used for bad it often turns on the one who utters it.

One Mantra, or Sacred Invocation is 'Om Mani Padmi Hum,' or, as the Indians say 'Ram Ram Ram.'

It should be realised that all sounds and words can influence matter, can even influence inanimate objects. Probably everyone has heard of the statement 'Mind over matter.' Well, it is correct, Mantras influence matter according to the thoughts of the human mind.

MANU: According to some Eastern beliefs the ruler of this world is the Manu of the world, the Law Giver of the world, the one who runs things, controls things.

It is obvious that one Manu could not adequately deal with different countries with their different types of peoples, nor deal with different cities, etc. Thus, according to esoteric lore there is a whole series of Manus and lesser Manus. You may like to consider it in this way:

The world is a big firm with a lot of branches, branches in all the great cities of the world, and super branches in all the countries of the world. Then imagine that the Manu of the world (who is not God!) is the President or General Manager. He will be responsible for general policy, he will exercise control of all other 'managers.'

All the other branches in the cities or countries will have a general manager who, while being free to make policy within certain limits, will also have to follow the basic instructions of the General Manager or Director of the firm.

There is a Manu of London, there is a Manu of, let us say, Birmingham, Brighton, Hull, just as there is a Manu for New York, Pasadena, and Santa Fé. There is a Manu for everywhere, and there are over-Manus who supervise and look after countries as a whole.

If you went into astrology you would find that each city

and each country are under different astrological signs. We say that this country is under Pisces or Aries or Taurus, when actually we are referring to the basic characteristics of the Manu. In the same way, the characteristics of a Scottish Manager would be quite different from the characteristics of a Cuban Manager.

A Manu, then, is one who has lived through rounds of existence as a human, who has seen and experienced the difficulties of humanity, and then, by progress, the Manu is appointed to a certain country or certain city.

MAUNA: This is keeping quiet, not talking too much. Too many people tell all the world about their Yogic practices, or their operations, or the difficulties they have with their wife or their husband. Too many people talk about their esoteric studies, say with whom they are studying and why, etc., etc.

It is a pity that people talk so much, because to talk of one's knowledge dissipates power and makes a student have various difficulties. It is much like trying to drive a car which has got a big hole in the petrol tank.

People talk far too much, they really babble and babble. Most people take things in through their ears and immediately pour it out again through their mouth, showing that there is no capacity in their mind to store knowledge.

A student who talks too much proves conclusively that he or she is not progressing along the right path. Study is a private matter, one's progress is a private matter, so if you want to progress keep your mouth shut and your ears open. It is the only way to progress.

MAYA: Maya is that which deceives, that which obscures the clarity of one's vision, causing a person to have illusions, frequently causing him to have illusions that he is far more important than he really is. He may have talked so much that he convinced himself of his own importance!

Maya is one of the big drawbacks with which we have to contend. This Earth is the World of Illusion, the World of Maya, and we must get rid of our illusions and face reality before we can go on to a higher stage of evolution.

MEDITATION: Meditation is a system of putting one's mind in order, training it, developing it. Meditation is thinking upon a certain object, or subject, or matter, so that one may know all there is to be known about it.

One can meditate upon a plant, and then visualise the seed planted in the earth. One meditates upon the seed, and then one sees the cracking of the outer shell and the first tentative thrusting of the life within, the blind groping as the little tendril twists about through the Earth, rising upwards towards the light.

One can see this little tendril going up as a white thread, and then emerging through the earth and turning green or brown, growing, becoming adult, and later shedding seeds which may fall all around or may be swallowed by birds, or they may even be carried aloft on the winds to be planted afar.

We can see these seeds also falling to the earth, and in their turn being buried and growing again.

Meditation enables us, when trained, to seek for the inner motive, to probe into the otherwise unknown. It is not concentration, for concentration is a different thing altogether.

MEDIUMS: Mediums? Well, what are they? There are two types of medium; the back-street fortune-teller who might somehow, through a kink in her mind, be able at times to receive 'revelations' from the other side of death. These mediums are untutored, erratic, and not constantly mediumistic. They are in the same position as the savage witch-doctor who has certain psychic power, he cannot say why, nor would he be interested in knowing why, he is satisfied to have the power.

The other type of medium is the cultured man or woman who has advanced far and is perhaps on Earth for the last time. That person will be mediumistic most of the time.

It does not mean to say that a person is good because one is clairvoyant, or telepathic, or mediumistic in some other way. It just means that he or she is a bit different. One can have a singer who can have a truly glorious voice, but the singer will have that glorious voice no matter whether he be a good man or a bad man, his character will have nothing to do with his voice. So it is with mediums—one can have evil people who are mediums, just as one can have a saint's 'next-door neighbour' as a medium.

An evil medium is one who is a fraud, that is one who imposes on the credulous and pretends to have powers which she does not possess. Often she is a good psychologist who tells back in a different way what her client has just told her!

This must be made clear; a person is not a medium just

because he or she SAYS he or she is a medium. It must also be stated that a bad medium, as in the case of a good medium, can be either 'he' or 'she,' but mediums are usually like ships—classed as she, probably because of all the fuss involved!

A medium is merely a person who can be used as 'a medium for the exchange of thoughts from one plane of existence to another!' In other words, it is possible for an illiterate person to speak in a language which he or she does not consciously know because the medium is just passing on a message.

MEMORY: It is known that the human mind can contain a knowledge of all that which has ever happened on Earth. The human mind is something like an electronic brain in that certain cells store certain memories, but an electronic brain occupies a vast space, and the human mind has many, many vacant cells waiting for more information.

Mankind is only one-tenth conscious. The other nine-tenths is the sub-conscious, and in the sub-conscious there is a knowledge of everything that has happened on the Earth, a form of inherited racial memory, because into the sub-conscious comes information gleaned during astral travelling of that which is on the Akashic Record.

By suitable training one can delve deep into the sub-conscious and dredge up memories and knowledge which the person did not even know was there.

MIND: Before we are going to get very far in any spiritual matter we must be sure that our mind is clear. We must be sure that our mind is able to stand up to the demands which we are going to make on it.

To attain purity of mind one should associate with those who are of even temperament, those who are sane and balanced, those who know the truth of what they are saying.

One should show sympathy to those who are suffering and to those who are not capable of distinguishing truth from fiction. One can be understanding and sympathetic without binding oneself to such people; in fact, to be too closely associated with the wrong type of person would be to contaminate one's own mind.

The mind is like a sponge which soaks up knowledge. If it be a good mind it knows how to use the knowledge which it has soaked up. If it is a bad mind it just stuffs mentally undigested knowledge into the sub-conscious.

Later we shall give some breathing exercises which will help cleanse the mind, but remember, if you treat your mind well your mind will serve you; if you do not treat your mind well your mind will serve you ill.

MING: This is not, as so many people imagine, just a precious piece of ceramic which appears in some museum. That 'Ming' is some ancient ornament left over from the Ming period (or Ming Dynasty) of the Chinese Emperors.

The Ming to which we refer is that which indicates fate. The Chinese consider that destiny is Ming, Ming is an Order from the Gods above.

MING CHIA: The Chinese, before the Communists ran wild there, were great believers in names. Names were words of power, names could be auspicious or inauspicious. So Ming Chia is a special school of names wherein auspicious and inauspicious names could be determined, and so that it was possible to give a correct name for something which was of importance to the name giver.

The Chinese well knew the science of vibrations, they knew that suitable vibrations could increase the power of an object, thus they started their science of names.

MITHYA: People are in bondage here through the World of Illusion. People have false values, false beliefs, and false understanding.

All that matters on the Earth is how much money a person has in his bank account, how was he born—to what class of society. People worship false Gods, the Chief God is the dollar sign. People are able to contemplate travel in space with equanimity, but they are not able to realise that the mind is greater than the material, and that the easiest way to travel in space is through astral travelling!

Mithya is that state of falsity which has to be banished before one can attain liberation from the bonds of the flesh, from the illusions of this world, and so come to a realisation of one's true Overself.

Mithya is a good thing to put behind us, because until one can wake up and become aware one is wasting time and coming back to Earth needlessly.

MOHA: This is a state of ignorance, the state of being stupid, the state of being in utter confusion. It is caused by lack of appreciation of that which has to be done and that which has to be left undone.

Moha leads to sorrow and suffering. In overcoming Moha one

also has to overcome Mithya, and then, and then only, does one attain to the stage of.

MOKSHA : Moksha is liberation. It is freedom from crass stupidity, freedom from ignorance, freedom from confusion.

It is the aim of all sentient beings to reach liberation, to reach freedom from the bonds of the Earth and the cloying lusts of the flesh, and thus to attain that stage which, for want of a better term, we will call 'Buddhahood.'

No matter if one is a Christian or a Jew, a Moslem or a Buddhist, one still strives to attain freedom from the suffering of the world, and entry into that which we term Heaven, Nirvana, the Heavenly Fields, or similar. We cannot get to any of those desirable places until we have attained Moksha.

MUDRAS : Hatha Yoga has all sorts of queer exercises, some harmless and possibly decidedly funny, but some highly dangerous. The twenty-five exercises of Mudras should not concern us except that I personally desire to issue a solemn warning that none of these exercises should be practised except under the supervision and advice of a really qualified person.

The dangers are real. A person may have some heart affliction which does not obtrude in one's ordinary life, but if one tries to emulate a dyspeptic snake, then one is asking for—and will get—trouble.

Too many people make a cult or a fetish of some of these exercises, and by over-concentrating they can do terrible harm to themselves. What sort of harm? Go into any mental home and you will see!

There are numerous exercises which have some part in the process of raising the Kundalini, and just to give you some information on this subject let mē tell you of one or two merely as a matter of academic interest.

The first is Khechari-Mudra. This is a series of exercises which enables one to lengthen the tongue. It takes several months, of course, but when the tongue is suitably lengthened and has its muscles trained, it can be turned backwards so that it completely obstructs one's throat. The Adept—who sometimes knows what he is doing—stops up all his body orifices with oiled pads, and then by practising the necessary Mudra he can remain without breathing for many, many days. This has been proved under test conditions.

Another exercise, or Mudra, is that of Viparitakarani. In this the victim, or practitioner, lies on his back with his head on the ground. He then raises his legs in the air, following with the lower part of the back. He should support his hips with his hands, and then the elbows take the weight of the body. Sometimes people doing this waggle their legs round in a circle, but before doing so they should tie a flag to their ankles to at least make some semblance of purpose to it, or they could even tie a palm leaf to the legs so that they fan themselves in the process.

Another crazy stunt is Pasinimudra. The person who does this should be doing it for a living on a stage. Anyway, this fellow wraps his legs around his neck as if he were tying a scarf around himself. It is much cheaper to go out and buy a scarf than to pay the doctor who might have to untie you afterwards.

Yet another exercise—Kaki-Mudra is where a poor soul contracts his lips and tries, for some reason, to resemble a crow. He then sucks in air very slowly.

A personal point of view again—in the *real* Far East the only people who go in for these foolish stunts are the beggars and those 'fakirs' who want to make a living and have not the brains to do anything else. The people who do these exercises are merely acrobats, jugglers, and the like. These exercises do not really help in increasing one's spiritual understanding, and if you have any suspicion of an ailment leave these exercises alone, you will live longer—happier.

MULADHARA: This is another Chakra. This one is below the base of the spine. It is the site of the Kundalini.

Most people are content to say that the Kundalini is located at the base of the spine, but actually the Kundalini is located exactly halfway between the organ of excretion and the organ of reproduction.

This Muladhara is a Chakra of four petals, the lower the evolution of the person, the darker the red colour of the petals. In the centre of the red petals—where they join—in the fiery shape of a triangle with the yellow square precisely locating the Kundalini.

The red indicates lower carnal emotions and passions. The yellow, which actually surrounds the recumbent Kundalini, shows that the Kundalini force can be spiritual if raised properly. But if it is raised in the wrong way or at the wrong time or for the wrong purpose, it can be like a searing flame

84

which can burn out one's reason and leave one a gibbering idiot.

The Kundalini should not be awakened except by some experienced Teacher who really knows what he is doing. It is better to wait, if necessary, for your Kundalini to be awakened in the next life than to have to come back for a few extra lives through being impatient and getting your Kundalini excited for the wrong purposes.

MUMUKSHUTWA: This is a very strong desire to be free of the bonds of the flesh. That is why so many people want to do astral travelling, they want to get out of the body, out of the imprisoning clay, to go places and see things for themselves.

It is also a desire to get away from continual incarnations, a desire to return home to the world of the spirit.

MUNI: This is a person who does not talk about his Yogic exercises or what he is learning, or what his Teacher said last time, or what he is going to say to his Teacher if his Teacher does not show him what he wants to know. Muni is one who does not engage in idle chatter, one who can maintain silence. You should consult Mauna here to refresh your mind!

MYSTICISM: This is a belief that by dwelling upon things higher than this world one can increase one's spiritual status. It is reaching a super-conscious state, it is increasing one's vibration so that, while still conscious in the body, one's mind is able to receive higher truths, higher realities.

Mysticism has nothing to do with spells or black magic, but only with that which increases one's understanding of things which are beyond the physical human experience.

N

NADAS: There are various forms of sound. Sound, in fact, is merely a vibration, as is sight. We call 'sound' that which can be apperceived by the human ears, or more accurately, by any ears.

Nadas is a form of sound that is heard within, without the aid of ears. It is a voice of conscience, the voice of the God within, the voice of your Overself calling you, telling you what to do, and—perhaps even more important—telling you what not to do.

It is said that 'Be still and know that I am within.' The 'I' that one 'knows' in this way is the Nadas, the Voice Within. You cannot go wrong in your present stage of evolution if you listen and obey that still inner voice of conscience.

NATURE SPIRITS: Humans in their conceit and over-weening sense of superiority think that they alone have a soul. Humans think that only humans continue after life, after death, and into another life.

Many of the ancient races worshipped Nature Spirits. They were not so far wrong because there are Nature Spirits, and they are quite as important as human spirits.

A human is a lump of protoplasm which has a soul or Overself which tells that lump of protoplasm how to operate, how to grow. In the same way trees have Nature Spirits, spirit-entities who look after that tree.

Animals also have spirits, souls, if you like, and it does not at all follow that because an animal cannot talk English, or Spanish, or German, that the animal is 'dumb.' Many animals have characters in no way inferior to the best of humans!

In the astral world there are human entities doing their own particular job of work, and there are Nature Spirits, those who look after plants and the astrals of animals. There are also elementals, but elementals we have already dealt with.

For your own evolution, then, remember that there are animal spirits growing and evolving on different lines from humans, admittedly, but in no way inferior to humans. They are distinct and quite separate lines; humans never reincarnate as animals, animals never reincarnate as humans. They are quite, quite different lines of growth.

NECK: The neck is that narrow passageway connecting the head and the brain to the body, and if your neck does not work properly, then you cannot expect to have messages conveyed from the brain to various assorted centres, because if your arteries are constricted in the neck, then you do not get an adequate supply of blood to the brain. If you have pressure on nerves in the neck, then various sense-impulses are delayed or altogether obstructed in their passage from brain to torso.

It is a good plan to have some exercises which have a definite end in view, exercises to free arteries and nerves. This must not be confused necessarily with Hatha-Yoga or with occultism, there is nothing occult in this particular exercise, it just makes you feel better.

This is the way to set about it:

Sit as comfortably as you can in a hard chair of the type used in the kitchen. It must be a hard chair with a back to it, you cannot lounge in an armchair.

Sit upright with your hands on your knees. Keep your head erect for a second or two, and then turn your head slowly to the left as far as it will go. Make an effort, and turn it a little bit farther, because it will go farther than you thought at first. Then quite slowly return your head to the centre, so that you are looking straight forward again. Pause for a second or two, and then turn your head to the right as far as it will go. As before—force it that little bit more to the right.

Do this so that you can almost feel the rust falling out of your unused joints in the spine, do it so that you can actually feel the bones creaking. Do it several times, then sit upright again—Oh, yes, you will have slumped down by now!—and pause for a few moments while taking several deep breaths, really deep breaths, holding a deep breath for, perhaps, ten seconds at a time.

When you have done that for about a minute put your head as flat as you can on your left shoulder, put it so that your ear is resting on your shoulder, and when you can do that push your head down farther so that your ear is crushed. Keep it there for a second, then let your head return to the upright position. After a second or so do the same to the right shoulder. Make sure that your head goes down just a bit farther than is really comfortable. In all pauses between alterations of posture you should breathe deeply, and then exhale completely.

Now for the next step—breathe deeply again, and exhale completely. Then take a deep breath, and let your head sink as far as it will, so that your chin digs into your chest. Push it a bit farther so that your neck actually creaks. Let your head return to the normal position, rest a moment while you are breathing deeply, and then let your head go as far back as you can.

You must be careful in any of these exercises not to move fast enough or violently enough to hurt yourself. With practice you will be able to move farther, and farther round.

After these exercises sit up with your hands at the back of your neck, and massage your neck with your two thumbs. You will find that this will help you, and might even assist you to concentrate.

It must again be emphasised that these exercises will not help you in metaphysical matters, in fact, no physical exercises help in occult mattters. Physical exercises help the physical, unless they strain something, and you would never, never find an Adept in the Far East doing these physical exercises except for purely physical reasons. For occult exercises you must do quite different things, and that has nothing at all to do with the physical. Many people go in for absurd posturings, and delude themselves that they are great occultists when actually they realise that they cannot do occult stuff, and so they are doing the physical exercises and calling them big names.

NIDANAS: These are known as the Twelve Causes of Misery. There is no point in listing them in detail because they are just things connected with material existence, such as lusts of the flesh and all that sort of thing which seem to have been specifically designed to keep poor suffering Man, and even more suffering Woman, on this quite miserable Earth.

We should get rid of Nidanas as fast as we can. There are such things in Nidanas such as pride, covetousness, lust, anger, gluttony, envy, and sloth. These things are not desirable things, we do not have to put up with them, and with a little effort we can get rid of the whole bunch, and when we come to make that effort we find it is not so hard as we thought, and then we know we are well on the way to leaving this Earth-round for good—and it certainly is GOOD.

NIDIDHYASANA: This is a practice of profound meditation, the real form of meditation, the type which enables one to achieve results. There are three stages necessary; those stages are:

First one reads or hears. One may read a religious or metaphysical text, or possibly someone reads the text to us. That puts information at our disposal, information ready for the second stage.

Second, we have the information and now it has to be thought about. What information is at our disposal? We think generally on that information, we think of it and we think around it, and when we have thought so that we have a grasp of the whole basic subject we come to the third stage.

The third stage is, of course, Nididhyasana in which we take one facet, or one aspect of the information which was given to us in stage one, and was generally thought of in stage two, and then we meditate upon that which has merited our more specialised attention.

NIDRAS: These are ideas which one obtains during sleep. They may be ideas which came to us during our visit to the world of the astral. If we brought them back to the physical just as we received them, then they would be of invaluable benefit to us. Many composers of music are able to bring back to the physical world a memory of music which they heard in the astral world, and so they 'compose' a wonderful masterpiece which goes down in history as a classic.

Unfortunately, many people are not able to accept astral travelling and are not able to accept the ideas put to one during an astral visit. One's particular form of religion may not have mentioned astral travelling, and so the adherent of that religion may think there is something wrong in it. Thus ideas become rationalised into 'dreams.' The human mind, which is the biggest drawback of humanity, makes a rationalised picture which completely distorts what the astral body is trying to tell the physical body.

If one would keep a notebook and pencil by the bedside, and *immediately* write down ideas that come to one in the night, they would remember them in the morning. People say, 'Oh, it's so clear I'm sure to remember it,' and then they turn over and go to sleep again, and in the morning they have forgotten all about it. It is a pity because many wonderful things are told us during our 'sleep.'

NIRVANA: This is liberation from the body, liberation from the lusts and gluttonies of the flesh. It does not mean the cessation of all experience; it does not mean the cessation of all knowledge, nor the cessation of all life.

It is incorrect to say that Nirvana means existing in a state of nothingness. That is an absolute error which has been perpetrated through people talking about things which they did not correctly understand.

Nirvana is freedom from lust, freedom from the various hungers of the flesh. Nirvana is not even a blissful contemplation. It is, instead, a fulfilment of spiritual knowledge, and liberation from all bodily desires.

The state of Nirvana is being in a pure state, pure so far as lack of lusts of physical things are concerned. But even when one has attained to Nirvana—freedom from flesh desires—one still goes on to learn spiritual things and to advance in other planes of existence.

NIYANA: This comes from Raja Yoga, and it refers to the

second of the Eight Limbs of that branch of Yoga. It refers to the attainment of virtues of purity, physical and mental, and to contentment.

It indicates that one must have a certain degree of austerity before one can realise the profound devotion which is necessary to give to one's God. If one has not the necessary degree of austerity, then one is so busy thinking of one's own desires that there is no time to think of God.

NON-ATTACHMENT: This means just what it says—non-attachment to any material thing. The miser becomes earth-bound because he is attached to his money; the drunkard is earth-bound because he is attached to drink. If one has a strong lust or desire, then when one leaves this Earth one is drawn irresistibly back like a fish being reeled in by a fisherman, one is brought back to visit those haunts which have most of what one wants—money, drink, or what? One hangs around, a disembodied ghost, caught inexorably by the magnet of that desire which was not mastered during the physical existence. Non-attachment means self-mastery, detachment from the lures and lusts of living on Earth.

Non-attachment means release from the desires which afflict mankind. A person who has reached this stage, who has secured non-attachment, helps mankind and does not ignore their need for assistance.

NUMEROLOGY: Words are vibrations. Letters, sounds, are vibrations, and a vibration is a pulsation, or a wave, with peaks and valleys following in a certain order. Such vibrations can be given numerical values so that they can be identified.

Some sounds are pleasant, just as some smells are pleasant. Some sounds are bad in the same way that there are bad smells. If we give sound numerical values we can have a table which can be consulted to see which sounds are good or bad for us. So it is that people of the East have a Science of Numerology under which letters—each individual letter—has a number, and if we have a name we can add up the numbers forming the name to see whether the name is good for us or bad for us.

Certain people have found by experience that if they change their name slightly they come on to a harmonic vibration instead of having to suffer from a bad one. So people who know how can use their full name, or their initials and their surname, whichever proves to be most beneficial.

Numerology, however, lends itself to quackery, and one

should only go to a numerologist who has an established reputation because some of the back-street practitioners merely want your money, they do not want to help you as well.

O

OBSERVANCES: All religions have certain things which adherents to that religion must do or follow. They are the Disciplines, for without discipline it is not possible to have a controlled, sensible being.

Some call these Observances 'Stations,' as witness 'Stations of the Cross' in the Christian belief. As witness, also, various forms of procedure in different societies. In occult matters there are five basic observances, or, if you prefer, one can say that there are five basic disciplines which one must follow.

One must have a clean body and a clean mind. One must study one's own body in order that one may get purity of mind. Health is necessary unless one is going in for really occult matters when different rules apply. But to the average person sound health is necessary in order that the mind shall be able to resist the auric emanations of another person who possibly is not so pure minded.

I stated above that one needs health unless one is going in for really deep occult matters when different rules apply. You may be interested to know why different rules apply.

The average person in average health falls between a range of average vibrations, and those average vibrations make the person usually unable to reach a few 'octaves' higher, but if a person has some illness then the personal vibrations may be heightened so that one starts at a higher vibration than average, and goes to a much higher vibration than average.

You get the same thing in the case of a dog; a dog can hear higher sounds than a human can, as witness the 'silent' dog whistle. But a human can hear lower sounds than the dog can. In certain cases, then, and only in very dedicated people, an illness is an advantage in that it makes a person respond to a higher frequency of sensory and parasensory impressions. For all others, that is, for all except those who have definite—very definite—knowledge of their destiny, people should cultivate a clean mind in a clean body!

By following the right disciplines, or, to get back to our

key word, by obtaining the right observances and purity of mind, one can obtain the highest form of pleasure available on the Earth, and one can thus make great progress towards increasing one's spiritual stature for other incarnations.

We have, then, a clean mind and a clean body. The third of the Observances leads to the elimination of impurities from the body and from the mind, and the cultivation of purer and cleaner attainments, that is, one progresses along the path of spirituality and breaks away from lusts.

The fourth of the Observances exhorts one to associate with those of better abilities and stronger spiritual patterns than one's own. The more one associates with one's 'betters,' the more opportunity there is of some of the 'goodness' rubbing off on to us. The fourth Observance is that we should constantly strive to associate with those who can set us an example, and lead us along the path of purity and spiritual development.

The fifth Observance is that we should develop the power of contemplation. We should not rush blindly and come to instant, ill-informed decisions. One should think about a thing, contemplate the matter, and then there is the satisfaction of knowing that our decision is made only after careful assessment of all facts in our possession.

OBSTACLES: After one has considered the Observances and what they mean, and how they can help one, one has to take a look at the obstacles which are in the way of continued development. So, what are these obstacles?

People are faced with a problem. There seems to be no immediate solution to the problem, no solution, that is, which is easy and acceptable to the 'victim.' The person who is suddenly faced with a choice, both paths of which are unpleasant, or distasteful, or entail hard work, or 'loss of face,' usually comes up with some form of self-induced illness which makes it possible for him to say, 'Oh, I cannot do that, I am ill!' Or an onlooker can say, 'Oh, poor little so-and-so, he cannot be expected to do better for he is ill!' A major obstacle, then, is one's feeling of inferiority, one's feeling of laziness, and so a self-induced illness is formed which provides an excuse which is not much good on this world, but which is quite valueless on the world beyond.

Another obstacle is dullness, mental lethargy, or, more usually, mental laziness. People take the line of least resistance, they lack the ability to look themselves straight in the face and see what a scruffy little moron they really are. If people would only face up to the truth and make the best of a bad job, the bad job would soon become a better job.

A very big obstacle is excessive talkativeness. Too many people talk too much too often while knowing too little. Talkativeness is a sign of an empty brain. A person receives certain information through the ears, and immediately it pours out of the ever-open mouth without having any opportunity of lodging in the memory cells of the brain. People talk too much because they are (and not merely feel!) inferior. They talk to boost up their own sense of importance, they drone on and on endlessly about the most mundane subjects in a singularly monotonous tone and in a singularly uninformed way. They think they delude the listener and make the listener feel that the speaker is erudite. Instead, the listener usually thinks, 'What a boring moronic idiot!' It is necessary to curb one's desire to talk because talkativeness merely gives one an entirely false idea of one's own importance.

All these things are obstacles, obstacles to development, obstacles which divert one from the path of spiritual progress. We must at all times keep before us the knowledge that upon this Earth we are like passengers at some wayside station in the far, far country, we are waiting to get somewhere, and the more we add difficulties the farther back we find ourselves. It is, in fact, something like a game of snakes and ladders; you move along and you find your counter lands on the head of a snake, and then you get back a lot farther than when you started, but if you play right you go up a ladder and you get sudden promotion!

OCCULTISM: This is concerned with the knowledge of things which are beyond the ordinary mundane senses of the body. Upon this Earth we are confined to certain senses. We can touch a thing and know it is there, we can know if it is hot or cold, or if it gives us pleasure or pain. That is mundane knowledge, but occult knowledge is concerned with the knowing of things which cannot be known by the ordinary mundane powers of the world. That is, while in the flesh you cannot touch it, you can only be aware of it, and when one can be so aware of it one can have.

OCCULT POWERS: Occult powers come to us after years and years of training, and after lives after lives of experience.

In the East the number 8 is a sacred number, a number which

93

is supposed to confer various 'magical' powers. In the world of occultism there are eight standard accomplishments, but one cannot have occult powers unless one first sets aside all thoughts of domination over others. For example, the advertisements that say, 'Dominate others with hypnotism,' are doing a great disservice to the world as a whole, they are inciting one to evil deeds. You can only go in for occult powers when you are quite certain that you are not going to use those powers for wrong purposes.

The higher Adepts never advise students to try to do all the eight occult accomplishments, instead one should make haste slowly and progress by comfortable stages.

It is better to try to cultivate good ability on the mundane plane before going in for occult powers, because if one develops occult powers before one is pure enough to control them, they will control the person who develops them, and that can be a source of much grief!

OJAS: This is the highest form of energy in the human body. It shows in the aura first as a dull blue light, but as the purity increases the blue turns to a lighter blue, then to silver, then to a golden radiation.

In the purer type of person Ojas is stored in the brain where it stimulates one's advancement into spiritual and intellectual reaches which normally would be far beyond one. When one sees a person of this type one can see the golden halo or nimbus around the head.

OM: This is known as a word of power. When it is uttered correctly, and with the appropriate force according to the circumstances, it confers great benefit on the utterer. The pronunciation is 'OH-M.'

It is a definite fact that there are certain Eastern Adepts who can raise people from the dead by uttering a correct combination of sounds. It should be emphasised again, however, that one should not go in for tricks such as this without very special knowledge and without very special reason, because if you raise a person from the dead without knowing what you are doing you will revivify a person whose brain has deteriorated through oxygen starvation, and thus you will have a typical zombie.

OMTATSAT: This is another mantra. Saying the word properly sets a train of vibrations in motion, and so by repeating the word a few times and in the proper way one can awaken certain centres within. It must be emphasised again that unless a person is properly taught they will not get the correct pronunciation, and so then they can repeat the word until their voice fails and nothing either good or bad will happen.

We have various chakrams which are more or less dormant, atrophied, or 'asleep in clay' as one might term it. But by setting up the right vibrations through every molecule of the body we can shake free the chakram so that it has a chance to develop, but this can only be done when a person has pure motives, when a person does not want senseless demonstrations; demonstrations, materialisations, etc., etc., are, after all, no more than the toys or playthings of immature children, and children should not have the powers which correctly repeated mantras can bring.

OVERSELF: There is a lot of confusion about ego, soul, overself, and all the rest of it. Well, let us remember that we here are like puppet. You might refer at this stage to 'Puppets' under the letter P.

The Overself is the soul, the super-ego, the super-being, the overseer, the one who manages us from some distant plane of existence. The Overself is the real 'I.'

Many people have claimed to have originated the word 'Overself,' but actually it comes from a very old Tibetan word which indicates loosely 'the Man in Charge Above.' So when you think of yourself down here, you should think of yourself as a puppet dangling on the end of a string, the string which is the Silver Cord, trying to carry out the wishes of the Man in Charge Above.

If you are very erudite you may like to have the Sanskrit name; in Sanskrit the Overself is termed the Adhyatma, and in Sanskrit it is the whole nucleus, the whole power, the whole fount of our existence; it is the point from which all feeling, all senses, everything about us, originates, and to which everything about us returns.

PADMASANA: You will recognise this when I tell you that it is the familiar Lotus Position. You will have seen Eastern statues of Buddha sitting, and most times the Buddha is portrayed sitting in the Lotus Posture.

The Western person who is accustomed to sit on a chair, the seat of which is raised off the ground, and upon which one sits with the legs hanging straight down, may find it difficult and strange to sit as the Easterner sits; the man and woman of the East sit on a fairly hard substance with the legs crossed, so that the soles of the feet face upwards, and, of course, on opposite thighs. The Easterner in such a position sits upright with the spine erect.

In Tibet lamas of high degree sit in that position all night, they sleep in that position, and they die in that position, for it is part of the Eastern lamastic tradition that one shall stay conscious as long as possible when dying, and shall sit upright.

The Japanese Samuri sat in such a position when he was about to commit ceremonial suicide, an act which he believed would save the honour of his family.

The Westerner studying occult subjects cannot always sit in the Lotus Position because of convention or because of—let us be painfully blunt—stiff joints! No matter, the position is not of vital importance. The Lotus Posture is, admittedly, very good for meditation, but the really suitable position for anyone is that which is the most comfortable but which yet keeps the spine erect. If you want to sit with your legs crossed, do so, and just place your hands on your thighs. When you are meditating keep your mouth closed, and let the tip of your tongue rest lightly against the back of your teeth. Your chin should droop so that it is barely supported on your chest.

Your eyes should be unfocused if you can manage it, or if you prefer, gazing into infinity. They should not flicker or wander from object to object. The point here is that your eyes should not see.

If you sit as suggested here, and breathe gently and smoothly, and with a definite rhythm, you will discover that it is an excellent aid to relaxation. Of course—to repeat—you should sit with your spine upright unless you have some defect which gives you pain in that position.

PANCHATAPA: This I described in the book *The Third Eye*. I have been through this ordeal. Perhaps here I may again remind you that *The Third Eye* is true, all I have written is true. But let us return to Panchatapa.

This is a very severe treatment in which one has to sit in a tight—very tight—Lotus Position without moving, from the first light of day until the last light of day has faded and been superseded with the darkness of night. One is not permitted to move for any purpose whatsoever, one is not permitted to uncross one's legs nor to 'take a walk.' One has to sit, and sit, and sit.

Normally, four big fires are lit, North, East, South, and West, and the fires are painfully close to one, so that one becomes almost like roast pork. The idea is to harden one by severe discipline. It has been known for a very experienced person to meditate in that manner for seven days, that is, from dawn to dusk sitting motionless, and during the night hours sleeping and having the meals which were denied during daylight.

This is very good for developing one's powers of meditation, because if one does not meditate one is oppressed by body desires, etc., but if one does meditate then one 'gets out of this world.'

Naturally, it is not at all recommended that Westerners shall do a thing like this because it demands intensive training.

PANDIT: A lot of people are vastly impressed when they hear of Pandit This or Pandit That.

A person may call himself 'Pundit' instead, but whether it is Pandit or Pundit, or Pundit or Pandit, it is precisely the same.

Pundit is an Eastern name for one who has thoroughly studied the Scriptures and various religious books. You might say that in the Christian religion it approximates to a lay preacher and no more. In other words, a lay preacher is able to do certain offices in the Church, but he is still not a preacher—not an ordained preacher, and a Pundit or Pandit occupies much the same status, or lack of status.

PARA: This usually has a prefix 'the,' so it becomes 'the para.' It just means that it is referring to that which is beyond the Eightfold Path. To make it clearer regard it as being supreme, beyond.

We have Para-bhakti. This indicates that one offers one's

devotion to the God whom one worships. It means a devout person.

Another use for para is in Para-vidya. This combination word refers to and means supreme knowledge.

If you were in India you would find that the Brahmins are the most consistent users of Para-vidya, they have almost a monopoly of the word, using it far more than any other religious adherents, because to them it indicates the great, the pure, the supreme knowledge which was Brahman's.

PARAMATMA: This is another word with our old friend 'para.' In this case it refers to the Supreme Self, the Supreme Atma, that which is us far above the flesh. It is our own personal Overself, that which controls the human body when on Earth and on other planets.

It is much more convenient to say 'Overself,' because names such as Paramatma, Atma, or Jivatma merely lead to confusion.

PATH: In Eastern lore this is referred to as 'The Path.' To the Buddhist 'The Path' is also known as the 'Noble Eightfold Path.' It is a way of life, that behaviour, or abstinence from behaviour, which leads to release from reincarnating, and thus eventually to release from suffering. For as long as there is life in the body there is suffering, or the possibility of suffering.

The Noble Eightfold Path is a code of living, and although it is often called 'a religion,' actually it merely guides the manner in which the right-thinking person should conduct himself during life. If one considers the Christian religion, Christianity is a religion, but the Ten Commandments would not necessarily be 'a religion,' but a code of conduct, the following of which would make one a worthy exponent or adherent of that religious belief.

The Eight Stages of the Noble Eightfold Path are:

1. Correct understanding.
2. Correct motive.
3. Correct speech.
4. Correct conduct.
5. Correct living.
6. Correct effort.
7. Correct intellectual activity.
8. Correct contemplation.

When you can do all that correctly you will find that life will be very hard for you, because it will mean that you are on your last incarnation, and during one's last incarnation there is always suffering and loss because at such time one is clearing up the odds and ends necessary before one can move on with a clear conscience and with no bills outstanding.

PEACE: Peace is the absence of conflict internally and externally. Peace is when oneself and one's surroundings are in harmony instead of being in a state of conflict. Many of those who are stated to be 'peaceful' are having an interlude, or rest, in a whole series of lives. For them—they are just marking time —things go peacefully like a deep and placid pool, unruffled on the surface. But it is not a good sign when one's whole life is too peaceful, it shows that one is not making much progress! If one is to meditate successfully one must avoid inner conflict, although the Adept can meditate successfully even when there is outer conflict; an Adept can actually meditate when surrounded by the enthusiastic members of a brass band who are putting out their Saturday night best. Such an exercise is not to be recommended because, unless one has reached a certain stage, it can be an upsetting process.

PERCEPTION: We have to 'perceive' before we can attain any knowledge. For example, a student first listens to that which he is told. Secondly, he considers that which he has been told, and from the information then at his disposal he forms his own judgement, reaches his own conclusions, and has a few ideas of his own.

Thirdly, the person who has passed through the two previous stages, and thus is no longer a student, has now reached the stage where he can perceive things at first hand without being told or assisted by others.

Probably he has now advanced sufficiently so that he can reach out from the body and visit astrally the 'Hall of Memories,' where he can consult the Akashic Record for the past, the present, and the probabilities for the future. When a person has reached that stage he is stated to have reached the Age of Perception.

PINGALA: This is a channel on the right side of the spinal cord. It contains sensory and motor fibres which have a bearing on one's physical life as well as on one's metaphysical life.

The Ida is a similar tube, or column, and when the Pingala and the Ida can be controlled freely by the person in whom they are located, time, material, and distance have no meaning, and are no longer a bar or a restraint. One is then in the happy position of being able to say, 'Prison bars do not a cage make.'

The person with such abilities can accomplish conscious astral travelling, telepathy, clairvoyance, and under suitable conditions levitation as well.

PLANES OF EXISTENCE (*Puppets*): Many people are not able to understand what they are and why they are. They wonder why such an all-powerful person as the Overself shall be constrained to deal with just one poor puny little human. Well, it is not so simple as that!

The Overself is like a puppet master. Just as the manipulator of puppets can manage the strings of several puppets at once, so can the Overself manage the Silver Cords of quite a number of different people. A person can be in England and have another person in Africa, Australia, or even on another planet; they can all be under the control of the same Overself.

We might say that these are like inhabitants of parallel worlds, because according to some beliefs everything that has ever happened, and ever is going to happen, has a common denominator. The past, the present, and the future are one. It is like being on the ground in a street, you cannot see round the corner, and so that which is coming round the corner is in the future to you. But if you go up in a helicopter you can see that which is approaching the corner, so you can see the future clearly.

Throughout history there have been cases where men or women have suddenly been 'possessed,' and have done things for which they were normally quite unfitted. Consider the case of Joan of Arc: Here there was a young girl who spent a lot of time alone, it was stated that she heard voices, and those voices exhorted her to lead her country. She did so, she became as a man, wearing armour, leading men into battle.

Do you know what really happened? The strings of the puppets became entangled. Joan of Arc, a young girl, had her Silver Cord entangled with a person perhaps in another country, perhaps on another planet, who had to do certain things. Joan rationalised and made the voices say the things which applied to her own conditions. One cannot help wondering what happened to the young man who was going to lead his country. Did he become as a young girl, spending much time alone daydreaming?

There are parallel worlds, there are worlds which we cannot

see because they are of a different vibration. We can see light, but we cannot see radio waves, and yet they travel at much the same speed. We can see this world in which we now live, but what if another world is superimposed upon it? We could not see that world any more than we can see radio waves, but in our sleep, in our astral travel, we could visit it.

We have seen groups of people, perhaps a whole family, who were completely tied together, who acted as a group having identical interests, and being thoroughly miserable when one member of the group was away. These people, members of one family, they may have been all puppets of one Overself. Most of us, though, are one of a group, that is, we may be here in this country and we may have counterparts in other countries or on other planets, and that is why sometimes we have a knowledge of a country even though we have not consciously been there. That is why we may have a complete and clear knowledge of another planet.

PLEASURES and PAIN: Mechanisms have governors, speed controllers. A gramophone, as an illustration, has a governor or controller which limits its speed and keeps it constant so that the record turns at the correct speed and plays music at the right pitch.

Humans also have governors, and the governors or controllers of a human being are, at one end, pleasure, and at the opposite end, pain. The average human lives somewhere between the two extremes; he learns to avoid pain in order that he may experience pleasure through the lack of pain. He learns also, to his regret, that some pleasures cause pain. In the early stages of Man there is lethargy and an unwillingness to make any effort, there is desire to do nothing. The savage will not hunt food unless he first be assailed by the pangs of hunger. Having discovered that food brings pleasure, he tends to over-eat, but then he finds that over-eating causes pain.

Pleasure, pain, pleasure, pain. The cycle of pleasure alternating with pain teaches one that which can be and that which cannot be. By having pleasure which turns to pain a human learns to stop indulging excessively before the pleasure be supplanted by pain, and thus there is the start of a form of intelligence.

The Adept learns not to try for high pleasures or he will get low pains. He learns that he must maintain an equable temperament so that he is not assailed by pleasure or by pain. Thus he learns control of his body, and by obtaining control of his body he is able to do astral travelling, clairvoyance, and provided he progresses he can later obtain disassociation from the body so that he can be immured in a hermit's cell—walled up for years without any light—Then he may be fed every two or three days. The rest of the time he is disassociated from the body, and his astral form goes soaring away over the mountains, over the oceans, and over the lands. By being so disassociated he can visit all the countries of the world, and nothing is secret from him. He comes to the council chambers of the great as a soundless invisible ghost, who yet can be aware of all that is happening. But such a person is not permanently separated from the body until death severs the Silver Cord.

POLTERGISTS: There are certain elementals who specialise in causing discomfort to humans. These are called poltergists. They are mischievous like monkeys, and of course they have no reasoning power.

There are many elementals of the poltergist type. Normally, they have not the etheric power to move any material object, and then they seek to find a young girl (or even a young boy, although he will have less power) who is just entering into womanhood, a young girl of from twelve to fourteen years of age, who has a lot of etheric energy which is undirected and is about to be channelled into womanhood. The poltergist manages to obtain energy—etheric energy—from the young girl, and with that energy articles can be moved, for example, a chair can be overturned when no one is within reach of it.

It is not necessary for the energy source (the young girl) to be in the same room, although she must be within about fifty feet of the manifestation.

Poltergists only do manifestations when humans are frightened. The elemental, who is always destructive, merely desires to terrify a human, and the more frightened the human becomes the more pleasure does the elemental derive.

POWER: Every living creature, whether human, or animal, or even vegetable, seeks power. In the forest the creeping plants of the ground move across the earth to the tallest tree. They grow and climb up and up to the topmost branches, where they derive extra power from the sunlight. The plant grows, and in doing so strangles its unwilling host. Think of ivy around an old fir tree; strip off the ivy and look at the deep scores in the bark of the tree.

The strong animal seeks to dominate those of his species who are weaker. His thought is that in dominating he has nothing to fear, for if others are afraid of him they will be afraid to attack.

Humans seek power through the misuse of money, or by self-styled importance. Others seek power by claiming to be high in some religious belief, and by telling others that there will be various tortures, or torments, or sufferings, unless the weaker person obeys the stronger.

Those who abuse power should remember this: 'Let the powerful man be generous to the poor and needy, for the cycle of life revolves like the wheel of a cart bringing riches to one and poverty to another, bringing happiness to one and misery to the other, and as the wheel revolves through life after life, with each life being as a spoke of the wheel, so the rich become poor and the poor become rich, and those who suffer now shall have happiness and those who are overjoyed without helping others shall know the pangs of misery, pain, and sorrow. Thus it is, let the powerful man be merciful, let him be helpful, let him bring help and succour to those in need that he in his time of need shall have help from others.

But the real power while one is on Earth is the power conferred by meditation. By meditating correctly we can obtain:

1. Free access to the Akashic Record. This will give us a knowledge of everything that has happened in the past, not merely to us but to the whole world and worlds beyond. We will know, too, things which are happening at the present time, and if we have a reason for it we can see the Akashic Record of the probabilities of the future.

2. Telepathic communication with animals; a most rewarding experience, because animals have a high intelligence not realised by humans.

3. A knowledge of one's past lives, and the past lives of other people. A knowledge obtained by methods other an incursions into the Akashic Record.

4. Telepathic communion with those of equal spiritual stature, no matter in what part of the world they belong, and no matter if they be outside of this world.

5. Knowledge of the time of probable death which enables us to make sure that our debts are paid, and our conscience is clear.

6. Clairvoyance. An ability to see far distant places, to see happenings and the probabilities of happenings.

7. Meditation enables one to control matter. There is a power of mind over matter, and when we can do that we can do astral travelling, because astral travelling is a simple thing indeed.

PRALAYA: Scientists have just discovered what ordinary humans have known for centuries; humans and animals must have sleep after a certain number of hours, otherwise life cannot continue. Here is something which Eastern science has known for centuries—the whole Universe has to 'sleep' at certain intervals.

At long, long intervals the whole Universe sleeps, and that is called Pralaya. There are the various periods, according to Hindu belief, and after each cycle of those periods the Universe sleeps while fresh peoples are being 'designed' and fresh worlds are planned. Such things can be observed in the Akashic Record.

PRANA: There are two meanings to this. The first is that this is a Chakra connected with the cardiac plexus. This Prana controls the state and health of the heart. It is connected to that bunch of nerves in the heart which gives a shock to the heart muscle, and thus causes the heart to beat with a certain rhythm.

This form of Prana shows in the aura as a yellow-orange colour which tends to become of a reddish hue in those who have very strong desires of the lower animal nature, such as excessive indulgence in sex or in food.

The second Prana is rather better known to the average person. It is connected with breathing and with breath control. We will not deal with it here, because in Supplement A at the end of this Dictionary we shall have a series of very safe, very healthful, breathing exercises.

PRAYER: People pray every Sunday and forget about prayer for the rest of the week, and then Christians laugh at Buddhists for repeating mantras. A prayer is a mantra, a mantra is a prayer.

The purpose of prayer is to wake up one's powerful subconscious, and make the lazy fellow work, make the lazy fellow get busy stimulating those parts of our body or mind which will give us the power to do ourselves what we pray that others will do.

When we pray the message is conveyed to our puppet master

our Overself, and if our Overself thinks that that for which we have prayed is essential for the task at hand, then we may get some help in realising our ambition.

It has been observed that most people pray for material possessions and power, rather than pray for the good of others! PROOF: It is a sad fact that so many people demand proof of everything. How do you KNOW that there is a God? The answer is that you do not, not in terms that you could 'prove' to a materially minded audience. You have to take your belief in a God as a belief, you have faith that there is, and you cannot let it go beyond that while you are in the flesh.

How do you know that there is a 'next life'? How do you know that there is an astral world where we can meet friends and prepare plans for a better life? Unless you can do astral travelling consciously you must take that on faith also. People who have been to the 'Other Side' at will, and remember completely, do not have faith; instead, they have knowledge, they are aware of the certainty of that which previously was a matter of faith alone.

The Tibetan attitude towards 'proof' can be put in this way; That which is needs no proof. That which is NOT cannot be proved. Wherefore it is not correct to demand or to give proof.

One of the most difficult things we have to fight against is this continual desire for proof. Continually demanding proof makes it impossible for us to really progress. Those who can produce psychic manifestations can rarely do so under alleged scientific test conditions, because the general atmosphere of suspicion, disbelief, and dislike, inhibits the higher vibrations which are necessary to the realisation of such materialisations.

So-called, self-styled investigators rarely have the qualities or qualifications to investigate the occult. People do not have to believe, nor do they have to disbelieve. All that is required is an open mind, and a desire, a sympathetic desire, to investigate without being biased.

PSYCHOMETRY: A person who is 'a sensitive' can finger an object and tell quite a lot about it. For example: A sensitive can pick up a stone on the shore of some lake or sea. Then by sitting down and letting the mind go blank, the sub-conscious can activate some para-normal senses so that the fingers can convey vibrations to the brain which form pictures. All life is electric and magnetic, and anything that has been touched by a person always has the mark of that person in future. It is like touching a piece of iron with a magnet; you will find that you have partly magnetised the piece of iron. A galvanometer, or even an ordinary magnetic compass, can detect the magnetism imparted to the iron by the light touch of the magnet.

In the same way, a person who can do psychometry can touch a stone, or a ring, or a piece of clothing, and can describe scenes in the past of that article.

Such a person does not do it for self-gain, nor as a stage trick, but only to help others.

PURGATORY: This is not hell, it is nothing like hell. It is more like the Hall of Memories in the astral world.

You may have a silver teapot. With a bit of use that silver teapot will have got tannin stains inside, and a few marks outside. Well, if you think of selling the thing, or giving it away for a wedding present, you take steps to remove the dirt.

In the same way, when some human or animal leaves this world there is a very short stay in 'purgatory' where the soul, or Overself, sees the mistakes committed in the life just ended, and there are some astral faces which go very red on such occasions! This purgatory is not a punishment centre, it is not the local jail, it is not hell, and there are no devils who gleefully prod you with red-hot toasting forks. Purgatory is merely a place where you shed some of your conceit, some of your illusions, and where you face up to the fact that although on Earth you had loads of money, etc., and people were afraid of you, here it is quite different, you did not bring your money with you.

There is nothing to be afraid of in purgatory. It is quite a pleasant experience, really, to get rid of the dross picked up by living on Earth.

Q

QUALITIES: It is useless for any person to apply for a specialised job without having the qualifications necessary for that job. You would not apply to be a cook if your speciality was deep-sea diving. In the same way one has to have certain qualifications or qualities before one can make progress on the upward Path of evolution.

Among the qualities one must cultivate are those of stability; stability of purpose, stability of character, and stability of spirit.

One must have the necessary incentive to give one the drive to pursue the much harder path of doing right, thinking right, acting right, and being right. Without drive, without the necessary incentive of restlessness, one is like a vegetable, and no matter how pure the vegetable may be it still does not climb upwards very quickly.

We have had two qualities, first stability and second incentive. The third quality is order. Unless one can maintain order within that complicated mechanism which is the human body then one cannot make progress. One must have order in one's acts and in one's spirit, one must have the conviction and the knowledge that one is doing 'the right thing.'

It is better to do one small thing well rather than to do a thousand things badly. One should act instead of idly talking, for useless talk inflates one's ego and leads one to a false evaluation of one's own virtues and vices.

QUERENT: This is 'the enquirer.' One who enquires, one who asks a question, one upon whose behalf certain forms of divination are being practised. One may be using the crystal or the tarot cards, and the person for whom one is using the crystal or the tarot cards is 'the querent.'

The attitude of the querent determines whether the divination shall be successful or not. If the querent is sceptical or downright disbelieving, or if the querent gives false information, then that person's sub-conscious is prevented from realising the truth.

It should be remarked that the person—the diviner, if you wish—is not trying to catch the querent, the diviner is trying to help. It follows that a querent should be impersonal, free from emotion, and should put aside all fears and all self-consciousness, otherwise the attitude may weigh against the cards or against the crystal.

If, as an example, a young woman with things to hide tries to get a tarot reading she may erect an invisible barrier of thought in case her unfortunate past will be revealed. The barrier and that which she would conceal is indeed revealed to the clairvoyant, but the matter about which the querent is querying may be obscured.

Tarot cards and crystals, capably handled, can help one, but one also has to help in one's turn.

QUEST: We come to this Earth in quest of knowledge, in quest of purification. We come that by suffering (and we get that!) the dross may be purified from our soul in much the same way that ores are clapped in a furnace and melted so that dross and slag are set aside.

An Overself may have certain desires. It is much the same as you wearing a suit of clothes which has a spot of dirt, eventually you send that suit to the cleaners where—in its own opinion—it gets badly treated; it is dipped in various solvents, knocked about, shaken out, and subjected to hot irons, but it comes back sometimes with the spot removed.

The Overself sends the messy bits of itself down to the Earth where, it is hoped, that by hardship the flaws will disappear.

Quest is the search for purification of the Overself. Or, if you like ancient mythology, the search for the Golden Fleece, that which has no impurities, that which was clean and pure and spiritual.

R

RAGA: This is another word for emotion, for 'liking,' for pleasure. It usually arises from the memory of some pleasant object, or from an idea or a person. It is, of course, an abstract term.

There is another meaning for Raga, because it is a specialised form of Indian musical composition.

Arising from the first form of Raga comes Raga-Bhakti, which is the spontaneous flowering of spiritual love. Usually it is caused by some intense and unexpected experience or emotion.

Another form of Raga is Raga-Dwesha, and that is the liking and disliking of people. We sometimes meet a person whom we like intensely at first sight, 'love at first sight' it is called; or we also have the converse—we see a person and we most heartily dislike that person at first sight.

These sensations are things which have to be eradicated by the developing person, because likes and dislikes, without apparent reason, are a sign of ignorance and a failure to succeed on a spiritual basis.

RAJA YOGA: Raja is 'Royal,' so Raja Yoga is often referred to as 'Royal Yoga.' It is one of the four main ways which enables us to return to the Great Overself. Raja Yoga trains mankind to self-mastery. It teaches that one must not be dependent upon others but must master one's own difficulties oneself.

RECHAKA: This is the process of expelling all possible air from the lungs so that fresh air can be taken in when one is practising various breathing exercises.

We will not deal with it here because Supplement A is devoted to different forms of breathing.

RECREATION: Do you know what recreation really is? Re-creation, that is, creating anew.

A person becomes dull and jaded by working too long at one particular thing. A person may be at a desk all day adding up columns of awful figures. At the end of the day the person looks 'dead on his feet,' but then he goes out and 're-creates' energy, that is, he obtains energy by engaging in a fresh form of exercise, or pastime, or work. Recreation is necessary if one is going to do one's best work in any particular line.

REINCARNATION: Reincarnation is the act of coming back to this material world from the spirit world. The time sense on a material world and that of the spirit world is quite different, and so one can learn lessons much faster on a material planet than one can in the spirit.

People keep coming to Earth—or to other Earths—in much the same way as one goes to school; one leaves home in the morning and goes to school, where it is intended that one shall learn certain lessons. At the end of the school day one returns home.

As one works through one class one is promoted to another class until one has learned, in theory, all that the school can teach, and then one goes on to a higher grade of school, and from school to a college or university.

In much the same way one comes to this Earth, and then keeps coming back to the Earth to enter different 'classes.' When one has learned that which the Earth can teach one moves on to a different world, just as the adolescent moves on to a higher class at school.

RELAXING: It is essential that a person be able to relax, and few people can because they are too impatient, too anxious to get results without doing anything.

One can relax anywhere. Sit down, slump down, in a chair. Examine (mentally) your muscles one by one. Is your foot at the easiest angle? Have you a tightness in a calf muscle? And how about your back, are you really sitting in that position which it is no strain to maintain?

Examine yourself mentally area by area. Make sure that all

your muscles are slack—REALLY slack. Are you sure everything is slack? Then how about your face, why is your mouth pursed up like that? Why are your eyelids so tightly squeezed together? Relax! Relax your muscles. Imagine that you have just fallen out of an aeroplane and you are sprawled on the ground. You would be relaxed then all right! If you can relax all your muscles so that you are not under constant muscular tension your health will improve. Try it!

RIGHTS: It is the right of all mankind to be able to travel along the Path of Spirituality. People do not usually realise that 'All men are equal in the sight of God.' In the same way, all souls are equal in the sight of God, no matter whether they be black, yellow, or white. It is *known* that there is no segregation off this Earth!

Too often 'rights' are limited by a form of communal law which is intended to benefit only the members of that community. Tribal law was the same; tribes had laws which benefited only the tribe to which they applied.

The stranger is always wrong. The foreigner in a country is always the one who gets the wrong end of the stick; the alien is always suspect, always misunderstood, always penalised. The alien is that which does 'not belong,' and thus is an object bereft of the sympathy and understanding of others.

It is said that 'Blood is thicker than water,' but until the parochial thinking people realise that the person of another tribe or community has equal rights, until the people of one country realise that people of another country also have a right to live, then there can be no real understanding or progress on Earth.

RISHI: This is a Saint, or a good-living person, or one who has mediumistic abilities.

Usually a Rishi is a person who has in some way been responsible for the Sacred Scriptures of a religion.

Rishi—an inspired seer.

RITES: Rites are disciplines, and whether they be pagan rites or civilised rites depends upon whether you are referring to the other fellow or to yourself.

The Catholic Church, as an example, has a very involved ritual, and in all countries where pageantry is used it is with the purpose of attracting people together, of holding them by this form of uniformed discipline.

Rites are things which cause one to have a certain frame of

mind because in having a certain frame of mind one can be attuned to the reception of, or perception of, certain things.

ROSARY: Many religions use a rosary—a string of beads—so that the person who is saying prayers or mantras can, by fingering the beads, remember to say the prayers in a certain order or the correct number of times.

A rosary is merely an elementary form of calculator which tells the sub-conscious that a thing is being done in the right order, or in the right number.

Fingering a rosary often gives a soothing effect to people and overcomes that age-old problem of 'not knowing what to do with one's hands!'

S

SADHANA: This is a word which relates to various spiritual disciplines. Sadhanas are especially four means of attaining freedom from desires. It is also part of Dama (*see under* Dama).

The disciplines are freedom from lust and similar, and need not be detailed because this whole book is devoted to them!

SADHU: A holy man, maybe a hermit, but particularly a monk. A person who leaves a lamasery or monastery and wanders among the people is given the term 'Sadhu' in much the same way as among Christians a similar person would be called 'Father' or 'Reverend.'

SAHASRARA: This is the highest of the physical centres of Yogic consciousness. It is the seventh, and although, as previously stated in this book, there are nine centres, only seven are named in the West.

Sahasrara is also called The Thousand-petalled Lotus, and a clairvoyant can see this emerging from the top of the head like a fountain of golden light, and all the 'petals' around the base are of every different colour imaginable.

SAMADHI: This is a special state of being more than acutely aware of 'reality.' In certain stages, when a person has progressed far, one gets to a 'super-conscious' state in which one is aware of divine realities, which cannot be proven but of which one KNOWS that they are true.

It is also a special form of knowledge in which one receives spontaneous enlightenment. A person can be pondering upon the meaning of a word, and one can have a sudden flash of revelation which gives instantly and unexpectedly the whole meaning of that which had been pondered upon.

SAMANA: At the centre of the solar plexus there is what is usually termed 'a vital force.' It is an emanation which can clearly be seen by any developing clairvoyant. The colour is affected by the gastric secretions in the vicinity, and thus most times it is of a cloudy green, something like jade, or, when slight digestion is proceeding, it may be like a yellowish form of milk colour.

SAMATWA: Tranquillity of temperament, placidity of mind, an entire absence of discontent, dislike, or antagonism. A state of mind where one is able to consider dispassionately, without bias or rancour.

SAMSARA: People come to the Earth in a cycle of birth, living, death, planning, and rebirth time after time in an endless cycle which remains endless until one progresses through every sign and every quadrant of the zodiac, and learns that which has to be learned, learns that which liberates one from the ties of the flesh, and thus from the necessity of reincarnating.

SANCHITA KARMA: Many people regard Karma as cruel, relentless, implacable, but that is not so.

People can have a lot of their Karma 'set aside,' that is, put in cold storage to see how the unlucky possessor manages. Then, if the person makes progress and honestly tries to help others, his 'stored Karma' can be forgiven him, for as you forgive others their sins against you so shall others forgive you the sins you have committed against them.

The God of all is merciful and just, but with a justness tempered and modified by compassion. No one born of Earth is ever called upon to suffer more than is his or her limit. No one ever has to 'pay back' that which would be crippling. Thus it is that stored Karma can be voided, bypassed, discarded, if the person being saddled with such Karma proves that he or she is worthy of forgiveness.

As an illustration let us assume that a person has been very cruel indeed in the past; Karma does not mean that a person has to suffer cruelty because of that, because if a person is reborn and strives conscientiously to atone by kindness, then the Karmic cruelty is discarded.

SANNYAS: This actually refers to a life of complete self-denial. It is usually said in the case of a person who has entered a lamasery or a monastery and who has dedicated the whole of his life to the attainment of knowledge. Here again he cannot progress unless he freely gives, unless he is willing to sacrifice that which he wanted for himself and give it for the good of others. This is the last of the four stages into which the life of an individual is divided.

There is a second meaning of Sannyas, and it is an initiation during which a person preparing to be a monk takes the final vows of complete renunciation and withdrawal from the world.
SARASVATI: Most religions have 'a Divine Mother.' There is a Divine Mother of the Christian belief, a Divine Mother of the Lamastic belief, and a Divine Mother as a consort of Brahma.

Sarasvati is the Goddess of Learning and the Patron Saint of the Arts.
SAT: This in a Western term could be likened to absolute existence, or a pure Being not upon the Earth. It is the reality, the Overself, that which we shall become if we behave ourselves and wait long enough.
SATYA: This means truthfulness, and abstention from deceiving others. It is known as the Second of the Abstinencies. One must be completely truthful, completely honest with oneself, as with others, if one is to make progress.
SATYA YUGA: This is the first of the four-world periods. Various religions divide world periods into a certain number of years, and Satya Yuga, also known as Krita, divides the periods into 1,728,000 years.
SEANCES: It is surprisingly easy to get in touch with 'the Other Side.' It is surprisingly easy to get in touch with elementals who pretend to be one's dearly departed friend or relative.

There are certain people, not necessarily evolved, not necessarily good, not necessarily bad, but certain people who, through some quirk of metabolism, can raise their vibrations so that it approximates to the harmonic of a fundamental vibration of some entity in the astral world. It may be that the person, who is then called 'a medium' (a medium for communication), receives information from some person who has recently, or not so recently, left the world.

It is highly dangerous to use such messages unless the medium is extremely well known, that is, unless you know that the medium is beyond suspicion. By this it is not meant that the medium will necessarily cheat you, but she may not have the intellectual or educational attainments which will enable her to discriminate between that which is fraudulent and that which is genuine.

In general people who have passed beyond this life are far too busy to send senseless messages, they have a job to do, perhaps preparing for a fresh incarnation. So Aunt Fanny will not come back and remind you to water the flowers, or tell you that her long-lost Will is in the third drawer down of the old tallboy!

SHAKTI: Here again we have the Mother of the Universe. The Mother is the principle of Primal Energy. She is that which creates, preserves and ends the Universe. It is, also, the forces seen in the manifested Universe.

The world here is a negative world, so the negative principle is the feminine principle. When we move beyond this world we move to a positive world, we move, in terms of esoteric lore, to the God-world. Here on Earth we are in the Goddess-world, the negative principle.

The powers which come from the Goddess principle are those to do with clairvoyance, clairaudience, telepathy, psychometry, and similar, and these powers also embrace those which are thought pictures which arise without thought activity.

A third power which comes from the female principle here, is the power of sound, the power of vocal expression, the power of composing music.

It is a Hindu belief that one has to know of the grace of the God-Mother before the true aspect of God becomes apparent.

SHANTI: In lamaseries and Buddhist monasteries the word Shanti, which means peace, will be repeated at the end of a discourse.

In Tibetan lamaseries those who are having a meal are read to so that their thoughts may be distracted from the merely physical aspect of food. At the end of the reading the Lector will often say three times, 'Om, Shanti, Shanti, Shanti.' It merely means that it is an exhortation to peace much as in certain Christian monasteries the words, 'Pax vobiscum' are repeated, meaning 'Peace be with you.'

SHATSAMPATTI: A person who is studying with an advanced Guru, with the aim of securing liberation from the lusts and desires of the flesh, will be taught in the main six things, which are:

1. Shama, which is the ability to remain tranquil and to direct one's thoughts, to control the mind so that the lusts of the body are set aside.

2. Dama. This is a system of Disciplines which enables one to control the body after the mind has been raised to a state when body desires can be exorcised.

3. Uparati. This system teaches one not to desire the possessions of one's neighbour. It teaches one to become circumspect in choosing one's associates and one's possessions; it teaches one to be content with what one has.

4. Titiksha. This is the ability to endure cheerfully and patiently the difficulties which are thrust upon us by our evolving Karma.

5. Shraddha. Under this system one has to be sincere and honest with oneself and with others. One must tear away the illusions and the falsity which surround one. In Western terms it implies that one should cease to be a 'Walter Mitty.'

6. Samadhana. Here one is able to concentrate one's forces, one's abilities, to a single purpose. One is not turned aside by temporary distractions. Instead, one pursues a steadfast path straight ahead to secure freedom from reincarnating.

SHENG JEN: This is what the Chinese call a wise man, one who has studied much, a sage, a good man, one who can control others with kindness and maintain discipline by kindness rather than by force. From it we have

SHENG WANG: Which is an ideal ruler, one who has inner wisdom together with the ability to be a good ruler.

SHIH FEI: This is the opposites, right and wrong, truth and lies or errors. That which is correct and that which is incorrect.

SHIVA: This is a word with many meanings. In the Hindu trinity of Gods it means the God who dissolves us from the Earth, the power called the destroyer which releases humans from the earth-body. It is a 'God' venerated by Yogis who seek release from the flesh.

We have three forms, which is birth, life, and death. There is a 'God' which determines when we shall be born. There is a 'God' which supervises us during life, and there is a 'God' (Shiva) which gives us release from Earth in the form of death.

SIDDHA: This is one who has progressed through the various cycles of incarnations, and is now a 'Perfect Soul,' one who has not yet reached the stage of actual Divinity, but who is progressing and is therefore at the stage of semi-Divinity.

From this word we have

SIDDHI: This means spiritual perfection. It also means that one has considerable occult power.

SILVER CORD: Just as the new-born child is connected to its mother by the umbilical cord, so are we connected to our Over-self by the Silver Cord. Just as the puppet is connected to the puppet master by a bit of string, so are we connected to our puppet master by the Silver Cord.

The Silver Cord has its name because, being composed of rapidly rotating particles of all the colours in existence, it appears to be silver. The myriad colours reflect to the clairvoyant as a pure bluish-white silver.

This cord is infinitely extensible, and it has no limitations. When a person is doing astral travel, the inner body separates from the outer sheath of flesh and floats away at the end of the Silver Cord in much the same way that you can let a kite up at the end of a cord. When the body demands the astral body, the latter is reeled in just the same way as a kite is reeled in.

Everything that we do on Earth is transmitted to the Over-self by way of the Silver Cord. Anything the Overself wants to tell us is transmitted downwards to the sub-conscious, where the information is stored until we want it, transmitted downwards by way of the Silver Cord.

When we come to death, then the Silver Cord thins and parts; just as a baby 'dies' to its mother when the umbilical cord is severed, so does the flesh body die to the Overself when the Silver Cord be severed 'and the Golden Bowl be shattered.' The Golden Bowl, of course, is the nimbus or higher etheric force which surrounds the head during life and departs at the moment of death.

SIN: What is sin? Sin is that which a group of priests at any time consider to be undesirable. Actually it is a rather meaningless term. At present procreation seems to be rather a sin, because it is stated that children are born in sin. How can they be? Without procreation there would be no race and no priests.

'Sins' include pride, covetousness, lust, anger, gluttony, envy, and laziness. These are the main sins, the parent sins, and all others derive from them.

Pride, of course, is only a misunderstanding of our abilities. Covetousness disappears when the coveted article has been obtained. Lust is another name for the sexual drive without which the race would not continue, and sex was held out in days of old as a reward by the priests for those who obeyed the priests.

Sex, in fact, now regarded as a major sin, used to be much favoured by the priesthood for attracting the populace to the temples. The priests used to stage shows which would make anyone's eyes fairly stick out nowadays. The priests also used to make it a law that every unmarried woman in the land should once a year prostitute herself to any man who in the temple grounds offered her money.

Sin is that which has been adjudged by the priesthood to be something which can weaken their own force, weaken their own power. The best way to avoid sin is to rigidly adhere to the rule 'Do as you would be done by.' If you wouldn't like it to be done to you, then don't do it to anyone else. Do that, live by that, and you are safe.

SOUL: A much misunderstood word. It is our Ego, our Overself, our puppet master, the real 'I.' That spirit which is using our flesh body in order to learn things on Earth which could not be learnt in the spirit world.

SPHOTA: This is something, perhaps a thought, or some special sound (such as 'Om'), which makes the mind open like a blossom in the sunlight. It is something which stimulates our mind to unexpected awareness. It is that for which we strive upon Earth in order that we may become enlightened beings.

SPONGES: You may wonder what sponges have to do in a Dictionary like this, but there are many people who are just human sponges, they suck up information which remains as an undigested mass inside the brain. It is useless information.

Human sponges are often 'do-gooders.' They know everything in theory, but they lack the application. They can only 'do good' in theory, they are not able or sufficiently evolved to really do anything to help.

Human sponges suck up information without obtaining any knowledge. They are tragic creatures who make a hard shell of selfishness around them, and then wonder why the world does not bow down in veneration.

SRI: This merely means 'Reverend,' or 'Holy,' when it is used as a prefix to a holy personality or a sacred book. Otherwise it is used in much the same sense as English people use the word 'Esquire,' or the Americans use 'Mr.'

SRIMATI: A form of address prevalent in India. It is the equivalent of 'Miss' or 'Mrs.' or 'Senorita' or 'Senora.' There is nothing mystical, nothing religious about it, it is just a generic form of address for ladies with or without culture.

SSU TUAN: This is the four essentials to humanity:

1. Being 'human.'
2. Having the right sort of 'righteousness.'
3. Having a correct sense of propriety.
4. Having mature wisdom.

STAGES OF LIFE: There are four main divisions of life. The first:

1. A child has been born, and through experience it develops and learns. The whole faculties of the body are being developed and improved. At this stage the person is able to learn fairly rapidly and without great effort.

2. This second stage is a stage during which a person takes employment, and gets married. The learning here is enough to keep the job, to get promotion, to raise a family, and to make enough money in order to prepare for stage three.

3. In stage three the person has retired, or is about to retire. There is more cultural activity, and more time to devote to the things which have not been attended to before.

4. In the fourth stage one 'digests' the experiences of the lifetime, and is able to send impressions along the Silver Cord to the Overself of all the gleanings of the life to date. The Higher Self does not start to profit greatly until the fourth stage.

STONES: Stones are materials which can exert a very great influence upon us, upon our thoughts, upon our health, and upon our fortunes. Thus it is that at the end of this Dictionary there is a special Supplement (Supplement B) devoted exclusively to stones, their nature, their influence, etc., and it is advised that you carefully read Supplement B.

SUB-CONSCIOUS: The sub-conscious has the greater part of one's make-up. We are only one-tenth conscious, and nine-tenths sub-conscious. The average human is not able to tap the knowledge of the sub-conscious, but when the average human ceases to be average and becomes an Adept, the whole of the sub-conscious can be examined for knowledge, and everything that has happened in human life is contained within the sub-conscious.

SUBTLE BODY: The Subtle Body consists of seventeen complete components. They are:

1. Sight.
2. Hearing.
3. Smell.
4. Taste.
5. Touch.
6. Tongue.
7. Hands.
8. Feet.
9. Organ of Excretion.
10. Organ of Generation.

The other seven include various items such as breath control, digestion control, mind, and intellect.

SUSHUMNA: When the Kundalini becomes awakened it passes through the centres of consciousness which are actually located in the Sushumna.

The Sushumna is a channel in the subtle body which is straight through the interior of the spine. It starts right at the bottom of the spine and goes right up to the top. The spine in effect, then, is a tube, the hollow part of which is the Sushumna.

Outside the Sushumna are two other channels; the one on the right is the Pingala, and the one on the left is the Ida. They coil upwards and later unite.

These three channels give rise to the Trinity which is common to most religions.

SUTRA: This is a terse sentence containing a general doctrine. It is a system whereby much truth is compressed into little space.

In the East the Vedanta and Yoga Sutras are the best-known illustrations.

SVAHA: This is a mantra uttered after a prayer or during parts of a religious ceremony. It means the same as 'Amen.' In other words—'So be it!'

SWADHISHTHANA CHAKRA: This is located around the area of the reproductive organs. It is in the shape of a Lotus containing six petals. In a poorly evolved, lustful person, the colour of the petals will be a very dark-brown red, a most unpleasant colour indeed. As the person becomes more evolved, the brownish part of the red disappears and becomes brighter red.

When a person is evolved the colour changes to orange-red, and the greater the degree of spirituality the more yellow there is and less red.

There is a hollow centre to the flower in which appears

radiations, the exact form of which depends upon the state of evolution of the person to whom it is attached.

SWAMI: This is much the same as a Guru. It is a Master or a Spiritual Teacher. It is used preceding the name of the person —Swami So-and-So—and is merely the same as 'Professor,' 'Holiness,' or similar. It is a title which is given when one has reached the stage at which it is deserved. If you want to be very respectful to a Swami you will call him Swamiji.

T

TAI CHI: The wise men of China used Tai Chi to indicate that to which we return upon leaving this world. It is the Ultimate, or the end of all things incarnate. It is reunion with one's Overself, and a state which upon Earth one can only liken to 'bliss.'

TALK: It is a sad fact that so many people talk too much, and about things of which they have no knowledge.

People get hold of 'half a story,' and they immediately rush away to their nearest and dearest and make a story and a half out of it, and complete fiction at that.

People should be like the three wise monkeys, see no evil, hear no evil, and say no evil; people should be like the wise old owl who believes that those who talk least hear most. Most people emit a torrent of sound like the falling waters of Niagara Falls, they babble, they drivel, they open their mouths and let all their rambling, unsorted, senseless thoughts come pouring out in a cocophony of unrelated sound, discordant sound, too. When a person is talking, a person is not learning, and if a person does not learn, well they come back to this Earth until they do learn. The best thing that most people could do would be to put a sticking plaster over their lips, and keep their ears wide open.

TAMAS: This is inertia, laziness, prejudice. It is that which enables things to maintain a constant form.

When we go to the cinema, or when we look at television, we are suffering from static inertia, and without static inertia we should not be able to see the intermittent flickering pictures of the cinematograph film or of television. In the eyes this static inertia could be termed residual ocular memory.

A person who is lazy or sluggish is a 'Tamasic' person.

TANMATRAS: This is actually five fundamental principles which correspond to the senses of touch, sight, hearing, taste, and smell, which we have with us while we are in the conscious state and which correspond to air, fire, earth, ether, and water.

TANTRAS: Tantra applies to any of the writings or scriptures connected with the worship of Shakti.

The purpose of Tantras are to give one a philosophy or discipline which enables us, through their correct practice, to obtain liberation from ignorance, liberation from rebirth through direct knowledge.

TAO: In the days before the Communists upset the human values, Tao was 'The Way,' the Principle, the Truth. Tao is that which shows us how to proceed, shows us the path which we must follow. It teaches us, in essence, to take 'The Middle Way.'

TAPAS: This is something which the aspirant Yogi has to do every day. It is a form of body conditioning. One has to do certain breathing exercises, one has to have certain mental disciplines.

Discipline makes the difference between a proud army and a rabble; discipline makes the difference between a genuine Yogi and a genuine fake!

Some people are not able to discriminate between truth and fiction. The latter go in for all sorts of absurd exercises, far beyond anything that is necessary or desirable, and they spend so much time flinging their arms and legs about, and getting in weird and unnatural positions, that they have no time or energy left for SPIRITUAL development.

TARA: I must put in this word as a tribute to Ireland! Ireland has ballads about 'The Halls of Tara,' wonderful songs relating to history of long bygone days.

In the metaphysical world, Tara means 'The Saviour,' but in this case the Saviour is the Divine Mother who was the Consort of Shiba.

TARAKA: This is actually a centre between and in front of the eyebrows, and if a pupil is meditating correctly he or she will be able to see, or sense, a light in front of and between the eyebrows.

TAROT: This is a pack of cards, seventy-eight cards in all, and the Akashic Record says that these cards contain the knowledge of the 'Book of Thoth.'

The cards contain—for those who can read them!—all the knowledge of past history, but nowadays they are also used for divination.

Tarot cards are shuffled, and one's sub-conscious magnetises certain cards in much the same way as a piece of ebony, when rubbed, can attract a piece of tissue paper, or in the same way as a piece of magnet can attract a piece of iron. The sub-conscious, which is nine-tenths of us, exerts a magnetic influence through the etheric, and so certain cards are sub-consciously selected. Tarot cards, in the hands of a genuine person, are genuine, and they are quite infallible.

TAT TWAM ASI: In a lamasery the students have to meditate on 'That,' which, of course, is the Overself, and they have to be able to distinguish 'That' from 'This,' the latter of which is the manifestation.

When the students are able to distinguish between 'That' and 'This' they are able to say with truth 'Tat Twam Asi,' which means 'THAT, you are.'

TE: A Chinese word relating to virtue. Virtue, of course, has to be moral, but Te also relates to power in all senses of the word. You can have power for good and power for bad, but Te most often refers to virtue and power used for good.

TELEPATHY: Telepathy is the art, or science, or ability, whereby we pick up and understand the brain waves of others.

Just as a radio station broadcasts a programme, so does the human brain—also a form of radio station—broadcast the thoughts of the person to whom the brain is attached.

Thought is an electrical impulse, or series of impulses, and thought radiates everywhere just as does the programme from a radio station. So any person with training can become tele-phathic, that is, they can 'tune in' to the thoughts of another person, and can also inject one's own thoughts into the receptive areas of another person.

TELEPORTATION: This is a little understood science in the Western world; teleportation is the art of sending a material object by thought to another location. A poltergist, for example, can pick up a large object such as a chair, and cause it to move violently across a room.

In the Far East, suitably trained lamas can cause a heavy, material object to be transported by thought to another location.

Gravity, which gives a thing apparent weight, is merely a magnetic attraction between the object and the core of the Earth.

Under certain conditions the magnetic attraction can be lessened, or entirely removed, so that the material object becomes less heavy or actually without weight. This process is adopted when an article is being teleported. It is also a system in use during levitation.

TIEN LI: This is Divine Law, the Law of 'Heaven.' The Law of that place to which you go when you leave this world.

TIEN TI: This is the origin of life, the Universe, everything. It is 'All-ness'; that which is and which always has been.

TOUCH STONE: Centuries and centuries ago, when the world was a much wiser place than it is now, before the age of aspirins and various tranquilising drugs, the priests and wise men had methods of calming a person who was nervous or irritable, or in some way 'off colour.' They made 'Tranquiliser Touch Stones.' These very special stones were shaped in a particular manner so that, by gently rubbing them, one could obtain a pleasant tactile impression which soothed a troubled mind, prevented one from having ulcers, and bad temper, and hysteria. You may like to read more about this under 'Stones.'

TRANCE: A real trance is the condition when the astral body willingly vacates the physical body in order that the former may witness some occurrence which can be reported back to some person through the Silver Cord and the physical body.

At times a person of mediumistic capabilities will be willing to have his or her body used by some disincarnate entity who wants to give a message. In such a case the medium sits in a position of repose, and wills the astral body to depart from the physical body. Then a discarnate entity can catch hold of the Silver Cord and cause the physical body of the medium to give a necessary message. After the message, or whatever it is, is finished the discarnate entity relinquishes the hold, and the astral returns to the physical of the medium.

Untrained people should never dabble in trance work, nor in seances, because it can have a very harmful effect upon the health. It is safe under certain conditions, but only under trained supervision.

TRETA YUGA: As we have said previously in this book, world periods are divided up into different phases. Treta Yuga is the second of four-world periods, and this one is of 1,296,000 years.

TURIYA: This is the fourth state of consciousness. It is not connected with waking, or dreaming, or dreamless sleep; instead it is a form of being super-conscious. One reaches such a stage when one is correctly meditating, because then one gets beyond thought, beyond wisdom, and into a state which is almost the equivalent of astral consciousness. In the Turiya state one experiences things not of the Earth.

TYAGA: This is the absolute renunciation of possessions and, what one might term, social activities. One who has given up or renounced all possessions, such as a hermit or a recluse, is known as a Tyagi—a man of renunciation. So—Tyaga is giving up possessions and social activities, and Tyagi is the man who has already given up possessions and social activities.

U

UDANA: This is a centre which conveys the automatic commands to operate the chest muscles. That is, it is our breath control centre. Actually, it is the bluish-white light which emanates from the pharyngeal plexus. The clairvoyant, as just stated, sees this as a bluish-white light.

UNMANI: This is the stage when we are out of the body, that is, when the astral body is withdrawn from the physical body, such as during astral travel or during a trance, we are said to be in a state of Unmani.

UPADANA: This is the material from which all things are made. Everything is made from a substance corresponding to the state of the thing which is made. A silver pot is made of silver, a glass window is made of glass, a human is made of flesh and bones, and nothing can change the fact that a human is made of flesh and bones. That is 'the Upadana.'

UPADHI: This is the ignorance which the Overself imposes upon the human in the flesh. It would be most unsatisfactory if all humans, irrespective of their progress, could remember all their past lives. Those who had been princes would be dissatisfied if they remembered their princely reign when they came back as an impoverished peasant, and the one who had been a peasant would feel a sense of inferiority possibly when reincarnating as a prince. Thus, it is that before a human soul incarnates he or she 'Drinks of the Waters of Forgetfulness' before awakening to consciousness in the body of a baby.

It is a wise provision that those who are incarnating normally forget (while in the flesh) what they have been in the past, although such knowledge is available to them when they get in the astral world by way of astral travel, and so can consult the Akashic Record.

Sometimes Upadhi is given an 's' and becomes Upadhis, and in that case it refers to the whole man upon the Earth and out of the body. It refers to his three bodies—his three basic bodies—which are:

1. The causal body.
2. The subtle body.
3. The gross body.

UPANAYANA: When a boy is training to become a monk of the Hindu faith he takes 'a Sacred Thread,' a symbolical ceremony during which the boy vows to observe certain virtues, which are:

1. Absolute purity.
2. Absolute truthfulness.
3. Absolute self-control and self-restraint.

Compared to the Christian belief, it is much the same as 'being confirmed.'

UPANISHAD: These are certain books which constitute the philosophical portion of the Vedas. These Sacred Scriptures deal with the more mystical matters, and the nature of Man and Man's Overself.

There are one hundred and eight Upanishads (a hundred and eight is a Sacred Number in Tibet). The chief ones are:

1. Isha.
2. Kena.
3. Katha.
4. Prasna.
5. Mundaka.
6. Mandukya.
7. Chandogya.
8. Brihadaranyaka.
9. Aitareya.
10. Taittiriya.

The Upanishads brought to a close each of the four Vedas, and so they had at the end of Vedas the word 'anta' meaning end, thus becoming 'Vedanta' which means 'the end of the Vedas.'

UPARATI: This is for which we must all strive; the end of all personal desires.

VAIDHI BHAKTI: Devotion to one's God, particularly when
there is observance of much ritual and ceremony, is known as
'Vaidhi Bhakti.' It frequently leads to an almost hypnotic state
of devotion to one's God.

VAMACHARA: In days of long ago the priests used 'Wine,
Women, and Song' in their rituals. Sometimes in Western
religions, particularly in Greece and Rome, such undoubted
attractions were used to lure male worshippers to the temples
where they would pay greatly for spiritual and other comforts.

In the East the use of 'Wine, Women, and Song' was for the
purpose of teaching the religious follower to obtain freedom
from passions. It was intended that he should see the influence
of the Holy Mother in all objects and all actions; it was intended
that he should see in all women, not merely an object of sexual
attraction, but the symbolical representation of the Consort of
God—the Holy Mother which is common to all the great
religions of the world.

In the East when it was found that such demonstrations
aroused the wrong passions, the whole thing was outlawed,
possibly to the great regret of certain of the adherents!

VASANAS: These are habits, or tendencies. In quite common
language, a man smokes a cigarette; the more he smokes a
cigarette, the more he wants to smoke other cigarettes, so that
in the end he becomes a chain smoker. Just as cigarette smoking
should be overcome, so should other undesirable habits or traits
which keep one Earthbound, Earthbound while in the flesh, and
Earthbound while in the astral.

Vasanas are often regarded as desires, but that is an incorrect
translation. They are habits which lead one to suppose that one
has certain desires, whereas they are merely habits, and can be
overcome.

VEDANTA: As we discussed under 'Upanishads,' Vedanta is
merely the end of the Vedas. Upanishads ended each of the four
Vedas, thus becoming termed 'the Vedanta.'

Vedanta is now loosely termed a philosophy based upon the
Yoga of Knowledge of the Vedas.

VEDAS: This is the origin of Indian religions. Special books
dealing with high mystical functions of the human body and

the human Overself. The Vedas are a source of inspiration which was in existence centuries and centuries before the Bible and before the Alkoran.

VICHARA: Various Vedanta schools order that their adherents shall engage in very serious thinking. It is necessary for a person to be able to think of, about, over, and around a subject.

It is also taught that thinking is not knowledge. Thinking is one of the drawbacks of the human body, for when knowledge is, thought is NOT.

VIDEHA: During life upon Earth, and during life on the astral world, we are normally in a state of growth, we are learning all the time. But we can also withdraw from continual learning so that we can 'ruminate' on the knowledge which we have so far gained. We can stop by the wayside and have a rest from the hardships and difficulties of learning. We can turn over our memories like turning over old things in an attic to see what needs to be kept and what needs to be thrown away.

People who are becoming aged often have what is termed 'a second childhood.' They live over past memories, they live in the past more than the present, they can turn back the clock of memory to see again all the incidents of their long life.

Videha is sometimes used to indicate Devas, who, of course, are humans who have secured liberation from reincarnation.

VIDEHAMUKTI: This refers to the state during which one is able to secure liberation while out of the body. While out of the body one can move wherever one will at the speed of thought, but it must always be remembered that when one is in the body one is able to attain to experiences which cannot be realised when out of the body. We come to the Earth, and to other planets, and incarnate, that is, we come to a flesh body to learn lessons which cannot be learned while in the spirit.

VIDYA: This merely means 'knowledge.' There is nothing occult, nothing strange about it. It is just another word in another language for our good old 'common or garden' term, 'knowledge.'

VIJNANA: This is what one gets after years and years of study, which is a very high realisation and spiritual appreciation of the God of all, the God who is above the Overself, the God who really is.

VIKALPA. This is one of the five kinds of ideas which exist in the lower mind. It is a form of imagination. We can have a thing existing 'in the mind,' and 'in the mind' it can appear to be very real to us. That is Vikalpa.

VIPARYAYAS: These are thoughts which come to one and which one immediately recognises as false information supplied by the sub-conscious. As an illustration, let us say that if one were to say that the streets of London were paved with gold it would immediately be recognised as false information.

VIRAT: This is the Manu who is responsible for this whole Universe. While on Earth one might say 'God,' but it is not God, God is a different Being altogether. Virat is the Spirit of the Universe.

VISHUDDHA: This is the fifth of the seven commonly recognised Yogic centres of the body. It is the 'Lotus' at the level of the throat. It has sixteen rays with a lilac colour edged with red.

This particular Chakra is connected with the will-power of the human being.

VRITTI: This is a thought-wave in the mind which swirls and swirls around something like a whirlpool, and leaves one in rather a state of turmoil until one does something about it. It is not a direct thought which comes, and is gone, but it is instead a thought which persists until some definite action be taken.

VYANA: This is a special source which supplies energy to the whole body. It is connected particularly in the male with the prostate centre, and excessive sexual activity depletes the Vyana. It is because of this that so many 'Masters,' who really are not at all, say that no one should have any sexual interests whatever. That, of course, is completely absurd. They might as well say that there is only black and there is only white, and there is no other colour whatever.

Sex, properly channelled and of a pure type, can send great power for good through the spinal channel, and can energise the highest centres connected with the spirit.

Depending upon the development of the person, the colour of the Vyana, which appears at around the prostate area, is from a dull brownish-red to a very pale rose.

WALL-GAZE: Buddhist monks, when they are meditating, try to sit looking quite blank, they try to have no expression, they try to be completely immobile, and so it is often stated that a monk has a gaze as blank as a wall!

WU HSING: This is a Chinese term for what they termed the 'Five Elements.' They are:

1. Earth.
2. Fire.
3. Metal.
4. Water.
5. Wood.

WU LUN: The Chinese sages believed that there could be five basic relationships, and that all other relationships sprang, or were derived from, the five main branches. The relationships were:

1. Between the King and his subjects.
2. Between father and son.
3. Between the husband and the wife.
4. Between brothers.
5. Between friends.

X

X as a letter is not prolific in the world of metaphysical terms, and it is mentioned here merely for the sake of the completeness of our Dictionary.

The X, however, has great significance in the occult world. It is used in the form of a cross to denote suffering, as we shall see later. It is also used to denote that which is radiating in all directions at once as opposed to a point, or dot, which is self-contained and is 'indrawn.'

The X relates upon the terrestial plane to all points of the compass, North, East, South, and West, but when used in the esoteric sense it indicates that we have to GIVE 'in all directions' to those who are WORTHY of our gifts. We must show others that which they desire to be shown, and that which they are ready to learn. We must help them and guide them, but only when it is clear that they are ready for such help and guidance.

A decorative and esoteric form of 'X' was known as the Swastika, and this must not be confused with the crooked cross of Nazi Germany which relates to treachery, warfare, and all that which is indecent and impure. The true form of Swastika—merely an alteration to the letter 'X'—has its projecting portions going the opposite way to that of the crooked swastika, which is as it should be because the crooked swastika is evil and the true Swastika is pure and beneficent.

The letter X is often used to 'mark the spot,' and as a form of signing by those who are unable to write. The X is also used in a different form, or different stylisation of form, to denote suffering in Christianity as previously stated. In addition, you will no doubt be aware, the X is used as an honorific abbreviation for the word 'Saviour,' and then it becomes 'Xavier,' or derivations from that. The honorific form is used because the parents of many people who are christened 'Xavier' feel that it would not be complimentary to use 'Saviour.' Thus the 'X' is regarded as a satisfactory and acceptable substitute.

There are two symbols which may be of interest. One is the point of light blazing like a star, which can indicate the One Within. The other is the symbol which is an X with small projections at the extensions of the arms which are shown rapidly rotating, and indicates the progress which has to be made.

Y

YAMA: Yama is self-control. It indicates that one has abstention from telling lies, abstention from stealing, abstention from greed, and abstention from lustfulness.

It is also termed one of the Eight Limbs of Raja Yoga. It is, in fact, the first of the Eight Limbs.

YI: The actual meaning of this Chinese word is righteousness. We would all, no doubt, prefer to do many things if there was some profit attached to it, but Yi is that which we should do without thought of profit.

YIN YANG: This is the whole force of the Universe. The Yin, which is passive and female and negative, and the male (the Yang) which is positive and continually assertive.

It is ridiculous to say which is the most important, the male or the female, they complement each other, they contrast with each other, they are absolutely dependent upon each other.

We cannot have a battery unless one end is negative and the other end is positive; we cannot use a battery which has a positive terminal only, it is an absolute impossibility. Thus, a woman is quite as important as a man, and a man is quite as important as a woman. The 'battle of the sexes' is a ridiculous thing which should be ended by an explanation of the dependence of each upon the other.

YOGA: The actual meaning of this word is union, or joining, or yoking together. It is the union, or linking, or joining of an individual soul with the Source of all Goodness.

It is also used (Yoga) to indicate various methods by which it is claimed such unions may be effected.

It must be made very clear that one can attain to such a state of union without knowing how; those who pry, and probe and fidget about, trying to obtain 'proof' of that which cannot be proven are merely delaying their own path, and until they can get a little bit of sense, or a little bit of enlightenment, they will not make much progress.

YOGI: A person who practises Yoga is usually known as a Yogi or Yogin, but if it is a female, then the female version of Yogin is Yogini.

YU WU: A state of 'being' and 'non-being.' The state of being in the world, of the world, out of the world, and not of the world.

Z

ZEN: This is a particular form of 'mental stillness.' It is not a religion, but a system of living. It is a method of attaining complete release from anything in this, the material world.

Zen depends chiefly on stopping the flow of 'mentality' by blankness of expression, blankness of desires, and blankness of thoughts, so that one is then able to experience and develop intuition.

Students of Zen meditate a lot, and success is achieved when *reasoning* is stopped.

In connection with this, it is worth mentioning that one of the biggest drawbacks to the human entity is reason. Reason, and particularly faulty reason, prevents one from perceiving the True Reality.

Humans often scoff at the intellect of animals, claiming that animals do not have reason, and that is correct. Animals have intuition, they have the ability to perceive a thing is so when not even the greatest reason-workers of humanity can get the same results.

The whole object of certain forms of Eastern study is to suppress, or destroy, or control 'reason' to let the true nature of the Overself show through and profit. But that cannot be done while Man is striving and scrabbling in the dirt for a few bits of grubby paper called 'money' which are of use merely upon the Earth. Again—Man has never yet, and never will succeed in taking even a single penny or a single farthing into the realms of Spirit.

BREATHING

BREATHING is the most essential of our functions. Without breath we cannot exist, because it takes breath—containing oxygen and other gases—to activate the brain and keep it working. But our manner of breathing is the coarsest way we can possibly use 'air.'

We have to know something about breath control before we can go to deal with any form of exercise.

Have you heard two people whispering, and you feared that they were whispering about you? What did you do—how did you listen harder? Now think of this carefully—you HELD YOUR BREATH, because instinctively, or through experience, you knew that in holding your breath you would somehow be able to hear better. That is so, is it not?

Again, suppose you cut yourself, or, if you prefer, imagine you have sustained one of those painful grazes which one can obtain from a fall on rough concrete. What do you do? Think of this carefully—YOU HOLD YOUR BREATH! You find, by instinct, that if you hold your breath there is less shock, there is less pain, but as you cannot go on holding your breath indefinitely you feel pain when you breathe normally.

Have YOU ever watched strong furniture removal men when they are confronted with a heavy object which has to be taken away? What do they do? They first look very glumly at the object to be lifted, then they dolefully rub their hands together while they take a deep breath—and THEY HOLD THEIR BREATH while they are actually lifting the heavy article off the ground. Instinct, or experience, or whatever you like to call it, has taught these furniture removal men, and in fact anyone who has to lift weights, that if they take a deep breath and hold it, lifting becomes much easier.

Does your work necessitate deep thinking? Do you have to ponder upon a matter—work out some form of solution? You DO? Then no doubt you will have noticed that as you think more and more deeply your breath becomes slower and slower.

An Adept who is deeply meditating breathes so slowly, so shallowly, that one has difficulty in knowing if he is breathing at all, and those people who are buried in the earth can suspend their breathing so that one breath might last for several hours!

Breath—air—is essential to us. Air contains prana, but prana is not a matter which the student of chemistry can shove into a test tube, or heat in a retort, or look at through a microscope. Prana is a different thing altogether. One might say that it exists in a different dimension, but it is absolutely essential for the maintenance of life because it is the universal energy of EVERYTHING. It is manifest in everything that we can think of, and yet humans use prana in the coarsest possible way when it is breathed carelessly, clumsily.

Prana stimulates our thoughts. Without adequate prana there can be no thought; without adequate prana there can be no healing, because for the latter prana is quite essential. A 'healer' is a person who can transfer his or her own excess prana to a sufferer. The area of its storage is in the solar plexus. The more prana we have succeeded in storing the more dynamic we are, the more vibrant with life force, the more we make an impact upon others.

There is no point in going into details about the ten Nadis, and how prana moves through them. We have dealt with such things and about Ida, Pingala, and Sushumna in the preceding portion of this book. Instead, we want to have some elementary exercises which cannot hurt us, but which can do us a tremendous amount of good.

First of all—how do you breathe? There is more than one system, you know. As an illustration, sit comfortably, preferably on a hard-backed chair, keep your spine erect and your head facing forward. Relax as much as you can while maintaining that erect posture. Now take a deep breath, a long breath, allowing your lower abdomen to swell out, but without inflating your chest or raising your shoulders. You have to keep your chest as it was and your shoulders as they were, the deep breath is taken by letting your diaphram sag downwards, so that only the lower abdomen swells out. This is 'lower breathing,' and if you do it properly you will find that your ribs and intercostal muscles do not move. Remember that, will you? This 'lower breathing' is the first of our exercises, so let us call it System Number One.

When you have done that, try another method. Take a deep breath while preventing your diaphragm muscle from moving. This time, breathe with the aid of your ribs and your intercostal muscles. Take a really big breath; you will find that now your chest is expanding, but your abdomen remains quite normal—unexpanded.

In this exercise you will observe that you have chest expansion instead of abdomen expansion. This method is termed 'middle breathing.' We called the other system—System Number One, so this time we will term it System Number Two.

There is yet another system and we will deal with it now. You are still sitting erect, still with your head facing forward. Draw in your abdomen slightly, as if you are trying to 'suck' it up towards the chest. Now, with your abdomen contracted take a deep breath while raising your shoulders and keeping your ribs and intercostal muscles as still as possible. This is a completely different type of breathing, one in which the upper portions of the lungs become well ventilated. We will call this system System Number Three.

System Number One enables you to take in far more air than the other systems. System Number Three proves to be the least efficient of the lot, with Number Two coming in between.

The best way to breathe is that using all three types. You start by slowly taking in air by swelling out the lower abdomen, and keeping your shoulders still and your ribs rigid. Next you swell out the chest using the ribs and the intercostal muscles, and at the same time you raise your shoulders and force them back. This fills the whole lung area and prevents pockets of stale air which lead to asthma, voice complaints, and often to lung congestion. It is an easy matter to practise this type of complete breathing, but you must remember that breathing in is only half the battle. When you breathe out—exhale—your shoulders should sag, your ribs should close in, and your abdomen should push up to squeeze as much stale air as possible from your lungs. Until we have this clear—until you can get rid of stale air and take in fresh—it is not possible to go farther in obtaining the optimum amount of prana. Presumably you have practised by now so—let us go a little farther.

We have to remember that breathing consists of three steps:

1. Breathing in.
2. Retaining the breath.
3. Exhaling all the breath.

There are various 'ratios' which enable us to achieve certain objectives. That is, we should breathe in for a certain period of time, then we should retain that breath for a certain period of time before exhaling over a certain period of time.

Let us look, then, at 'ratios.'

RATIOS: As probably everyone knows by now, the lungs are like sponges inside a sponge bag. If you fill the lungs with air the oxygen is taken into the blood, and waste gases from the blood pass back into the lungs and become lodged in some of the deeper sacs of our 'sponges.'

We need to exhale for twice as long as we inhale because it may be taken that it needs twice the time to get the impure air out of the lungs. At the sime time we should squeeze out as much air as we can.

If we do not completely exhale, then we cannot get full lungs of air on the next inhalation, and the incoming air will be contaminated by the stale air (like stagnant water in a pond) in the deeper sacs.

Stale air lets bacilli remain undisturbed, and so the lungs can be affected by T.B., which is not so easily the case if one breathes deeply and exhales completely.

The ratio of one unit in and two units out should be adhered to. As an example, breathe in for four seconds and breathe out for eight seconds. With practice you can breathe in over a much higher time and breathe out over twice that time.

We have seen that the average in–out ratio is one to two. Now let us look at the next step.

How long should we retain our breath? An average time is four times the amount of seconds it took you to inhale, or twice as long as it takes you to exhale. So on our former illustration you should breathe in for four seconds, retain the breath for four times four seconds, that is, sixteen seconds, and breathe out over twice four seconds, that is, eight seconds. So we have —breathe in for four seconds, hold your breath for sixteen seconds, and breathe out for eight seconds.

Naturally, this is just an illustration, just an example, for soon you will want to hold your breath for longer and have some different ratios, but we will deal with that all in its turn. You should keep before you, though, this thought; if you breathe irregularly, you are irregular in the mind. When your breath is steady so is your mind. As you breathe, so are you.

Now we will have some exercises which it is KNOWN will be of great help to you if you will carry them out conscientiously. To save time and paper, and all that, let it now be stated that for all these exercises you should be sitting comfortably. If you are young, and have some practice in such things, you may like to sit in the Lotus Position, or sit with your legs crossed, but all that matters really is that you sit so that you are comfortable, never mind about the exotic things, just sit comfortably; keep your spine erect, and your head (unless specifically told otherwise) facing forward.

We shall have to have some period of time—some unit—and just as in the old days of photography people used to count off seconds. 'Kodak One, Kodak Two, Kodak Three, etc.' (free advertisement for Kodak!). We can use 'OM One, OM Two, OM Three,' and so on.

Here is the first exercise. Remember, you are sitting on a hard chair with your spine erect and your head facing forward. Take two or three deep breaths—just take in the breath, hold it for about a second, and let it out. Do that two or three times. Now—put a finger against your right nostril so that you cannot breathe through that nostril. It does not matter which finger you use, or even if you use your thumb, the whole purpose is to close the nostril so that it cannot be used.

Inhale through the left nostril to the mental count of 'OM One, OM Two, OM Three, OM Four, OM Five.' Then exhale through the left nostril (be sure that you keep the right one tightly closed) while doing the 'OM' count ten times. In every case such as this the breathing out time is twice that of the breathing in time, that is a fixed rule.

Repeat this twenty times, that is, breathe in through the left nostril, and exhale through the left nostril twenty times, breathing in over a period of five 'OM's' and breathing out over a period of ten 'OM's.'

After that just sit still for a few moments, and see if you do not already feel quite a lot better, and remember, you are just starting! The second stage comes next.

You have just had your right nostril closed, so now you do the same thing but keep your left nostril closed. Again, it does not matter which finger you use, or even which hand you use. Proceed exactly as you did when breathing through the left nostril, take exactly the same amount of time, and do this breathing through the right nostril for twenty times as you did for the left.

You must breathe as silently as you can, and you must take what we term the complete breath, that is, using your abdomen, using your chest muscles, and raising and throwing back your shoulders. You have to get in as much air as you can, and you have to get out as much air as you can. After these exercises you will have no foul or stale air left in your lungs!

This first exercise should be carried out for two weeks. You can slowly—very slowly—increase the time of inhalation and exhalation, but do not do anything which strains you or tires you. You must 'make haste slowly.' If you find five seconds in and ten seconds out is too much, then make it four, or even three, seconds in, and eight or six seconds out. These particular figures are given merely as a guide, you have to use common-sense, and you have to suit yourself. If you start with a smaller time, then you will make progress but you will take rather a longer period over it, while being much, much safer.

Observe particularly that in the above exercise you do not retain the breath; that is done for a special reason, because this exercise is designed to make the nostrils accustomed to breathing properly. So many people breathe through the mouth, or through one nostril, and the exercise given above is a form of training process first.

We suggested that you should do this exercise for two weeks or so. If you take two weeks, three weeks, or four weeks it does not matter, there is no hurry, you have plenty of time, and it is better to do a thing slowly and properly because rushing through does no good. So now, after two, or three, or four weeks, whatever you like, let us get on to what is known as the alternate nostril breathing.

Remember how you have to sit? Well, it should be second nature by now! You are sitting, then, on a hard chair with your feet together, your spine erect, your head level, and your gaze straight forward. So you start now by closing the right nostril while you breathe through the left. Hold the breath a moment while you close the left nostril and exhale through the right nostril, that is, in this case, you are breathing in through one nostril and out through the other.

Next time inhale through the right nostril, and when you have a big lungful of air close the right nostril with a finger or thumb, and exhale through the left. Again, you have to breathe in for five or six seconds, and breathe out for ten or twelve seconds.

Have you got that right? First you close your right nostril with a finger and inhale through the left nostril. Then you close the left nostril and exhale with the right. After that you change things around, you inhale through the right nostril (with the left closed), and then you close the right and exhale through the left. Do that for about twenty times.

After a month you should be able to increase the time so that you are doing eight and sixteen seconds, and when you have been doing it a month, or two months, you will find that you are very, very much better in health. Your sight will improve, and you will become lighter on your feet. It is suggested that this second exercise be practised for three months because it is still a 'probationary' period, or a period in which your breathing mechanism is becoming trained.

Exercise Number Three: This is similar to the Number Two, but we have here retention of breath as well. It should be stated now that although one should retain the breath for four times as long as one took to breathe in, until you are well used to this system it is much more comfortable to retain your breath for only twice as long as it took to breathe it in, and then after a few months you can work up to the one to four ratio.

In this third exercise one has to inhale the air through the left nostril while doing our 'OM' count four times. Then one retains the air during an 'OM' count of eight times. After that, exhale through the right nostril (we breathed in through the left, remember) eight times. When we have breathed out, and without stopping, inhale through the right nostril (and with the left closed), retain the breath for the eight 'OM's,' and then breathe out through the opposite nostril. You would be well advised to practise this twenty times a day.

It really does not matter what finger or thumb you use to close off the unwanted nostril. So many people say you must not use this finger or you must use that finger, just to try to make things look mysterious. In my case I have been doing it for more years than you would believe, and I can tell you from personal experience, as well as from the observed experience of others, IT DOES NOT MATTER WHICH FINGER OR THUMB YOU USE!

You will, of course, be practising and getting bigger and bigger breaths, and longer and longer retentions, and slower and slower exhalations. You will be able to do, to start, four seconds in, hold it eight seconds, and breathe out for eight seconds. But after two months or so you will be able to breathe in for eight seconds, hold it for sixteen seconds, and exhale for sixteen seconds, and to really give you something to work for, when you have been doing it for a year you should be able to breathe in for eight seconds, hold it for about half a minute, and then breathe out over some sixteen seconds. But you should not try that until you have been practising for some twelve months.

This really is a very good system of breathing, and one which should be practised every day for 'twenty rounds.'

Here is an exercise which enables one to keep warm in cold weather. It is something much practised in Tibet where a lama can sit unclothed on ice, and even melt ice around him and dry off wet blankets draped around his shoulders.

Here's how you do it. Sit comfortably again, and make sure that you really ARE sitting with your spine upright. You must have no tensions or pressing worries for the moment. Close your eyes, and think of yourself saying, 'OM, OM, OM,' telepathically.

Close your left nostril, and take in as much air as you can through the right nostril. Then close the right nostril (your thumb is the best for this because it is most convenient), and retain the breath by pressing your chin hard against your chest, bring your chin up close to your neck.

Hold the breath for a time, and then gradually exhale through the left nostril by closing the right nostril (again the thumb is easiest here).

Careful note—in this particular exercise one always breathes in through the right nostril, and always breathes out through the left nostril.

You should do this from a start of ten breathings, during which you gradually increase the time of breath retention, up to some fifty times, but you must increase your breath retention very gradually, there is no need to rush, and while on the subject here is a little note which may free you from worry; when you have been doing it for some time, and you are doing it with deep breath retention, you may find that you perspire from the roots of the hair. That is perfectly safe, perfectly normal, and really does increase the health and cleanliness of the body.

Here is another system of breathing which is very good to improve the state of the blood, and keep one cool.

Have you ever seen how a dog or a cat folds the tongue so that it becomes a vee shape? Well, in this case we are going to be like the cat! Sit as before, that is, comfortably on a hard seat with the spine erect. Protrude your tongue just a little, and make it so that it has a vee. Then you draw air THROUGH THE MOUTH with an indrawn 'Ssss.' Hold your breath as long as possible, and then exhale through the nostrils. You need to do this for twenty times a day.

It is important that you should be absolutely regular in these exercises. Do not miss one day and do twice as long the next day, that is just a waste of time. If you are not going to do the exercises regularly, then it is far better not to start. So—be regular, be punctual, try to do your exercises at the same time every day, and when doing them do not screw up your face, do not indulge in any contortions of any kind. If you find that you get any pain, stop immediately until the pain is gone. Further, you cannot do these exercises if you have just over-stuffed yourself with food. Most people eat too much for too long to too little purpose, and so a moderate diet is to be preferred.

As a final warning, do not do these exercises if you have heart disease or T.B. Do not try to hold your breath longer than is comfortable. After all, there will be other lives, what you do not learn in this life you can always 'drop in' again, and take up where you left off! And it should be stated, too, that unless you are very young, very supple, and very well insured, you should not do any of the exercises which require you to balance on one thumb or sit with your feet resting on the top of your head or something. Unless you were born an Easterner, or unless your parents were acrobats at the local circus, you will be well advised to leave these things alone.

SUPPLEMENT B

STONES

THIS is a supplement about various kinds of stones, because they have great influence on the life of each of us. Stones are the oldest solid things on this Earth; they were in existence before humans were ever dreamed of—or nightmared of!—and will be in existence long after we have gone.

Depending on your point of view, you may think of stones as a collection of chemicals, or as a lot of molecules which wobble around according to the number of them crammed into one space. Stones, though, have very strong vibrations. In effect they are like radio transmitters, transmitting their messages for good or for bad all the time.

Let us look at stones, starting with:

AGATE: Many people regard agates as a red stone, but actually there are red, green, brown, and a sort of ginger colour. In the Far East the red, or blood agate, as it is often called, is truly a protection against poisonous insects such as spiders. This is not fiction. Agates give off a radiation which disheartens spiders and scorpions and makes them 'seek pastures new.'

There is a form of brown agate which radiates a vibration which gives a man self-confidence, and thus by giving him a form of 'Dutch courage' gives him victory over his enemies or success with his lady friends.

In the medical field it has been proved that if a person wears a brown agate next to his skin, preferably over his sternum, that is, hanging around his neck over his breast-bone, it increases his intelligence and helps to allay fevers and madness. From the latter you will readily observe that not many brown agates are so worn.

In the Middle East some people wear a shaped agate which is alleged to keep away intestinal infections which are normally quite prevalent in the Middle East.

There are black agates, green agates, and grey, but in China there is a very, very remarkable agate which has certain fossilised remains in it, and if you take one of these stones which have been highly polished you will see the patterns of small plant-life forms such as ferns. This is used by farmers as a decoration in the hope that they will have a very profitable agricultural year.

AMBER: If you have trouble with your kidneys or your liver, or if you are troubled with that civilised complaint from which our pharmaceutical houses reap a large fortune (constipation) take some powdered amber, grind it so it is like flour, then mix it with honey and a little water. Then swallow the muck, but only if you are within reach of the appropriate convenience of civilisation, because this is a remedy which really *does* work, as you would find out. The only difficulty is—amber is rather expensive.

Ladies who desire a husband and have not much luck in attracting them should have a piece of amber shaped as a phallic symbol. By wearing such a symbol it would attract a man who had the right desires for her. Thus she would get the husband for which she had such a desire.

Amber is a stone, but it is not very much used in the West because, unless skilfully polished, it is rather dull.

AMETHYST: Many bishops wear an amethyst in the ring which the devout kiss on the bishop's finger. An amethyst, which is of violet or wine colour, makes one tranquil. In other words, the molecular vibration of the material which we call the amethyst oscillates at such a period of frequency that it heterodynes with belligerent vibrations of a human and causes those vibrations to slow down and become tranquil!

The amethyst was used as a tranquiliser in the Far East long before aspirin took over that field.

ANTIPATHES: This is a stone which is quite black. It looks something like a highly polished piece of coal of the anthracite variety. It is little used now in the West because of its complete blackness. It has been used, however, as the background to a super-imposed cameo of ivory.

BERYL: St. Thomas is the patron saint of the beryl. It is stated that he used the yellow beryl for curing diseases of the liver. The beryl normally is of a green coloration. It is a stone which helps in the matter of digestion.

CARNELIAN: Some people call the carnelian a blood stone. It has a vibration which damps down the pulses of the blood, and it is truly a fact that if a person has congestion of blood in the head, the congestion is relieved very greatly if the frontal lobes and the site of the atlas be stroked with a smooth carnelian.

Carnelians are sometimes opaque, but the best ones are translucent.

CATOCHITIS: This is really a remarkable stone found in some of the Mediterranean islands, particularly Corsica. It is a stone which is magnetic to human skin so that if you rub your hands together and then touch the catochitis that stone will stick to the hand, provided, of course, that it be not too heavy.

The Corsicans use such a stone to protect them from being hypnotised.

CHALCEDONY: In certain backward countries (or are they really advanced?) chalcedony are used powdered. It helps to pass gall-stones. The chalcedony powder caused dilation of the gall-bladder and all passages connected thereto. Thus gall-stones which had been impacted into the wall of the gall-bladder would be passed out without an operation.

CRYSTAL: Crystal is a very peculiar form of rock. It is clearer than glass, and has extremely great powers in the field of 'crystal gazing.' Those who are in any way gifted with the ability of clairvoyance will find that this increases with the use of a piece of flawless crystal.

The crystal has a vibration which is compatible with that of the third eye, it strengthens the third eye, strengthens one's 'seership.'

In various parts of Ireland little crystal balls are set in silver rings, and it is believed that these are able to attract favourable responses from the Irish leprachauns!

Priests in bygone ages in the Far East would go out in their search-parties and find a lump of crystal in the Andes or in the Himalayas. They would carefully chip off rough edges, and through years and years would carve the piece of rock into spherical shape. Then generation after generation of priests would polish the crystal by using finer and finer sand and water, the sand being embedded in soft leather. At last the crystal would be ready for religious use—seeing the future, seeing the will of the Gods!

DIAMOND: The diamond is a close cousin to a lump of coal. It is merely a piece of carbon which has been given a higher education, in other words, it vibrates at a higher frequency.

It is often believed that a diamond renders one immune from poisons and madness. In the health line a diamond was believed to cure most illnesses. At one time in India the Koh-I-Noor Diamond was dipped in water and swished around with the intention of imparting some of its qualities to the water. As the person who held the diamond did not necessarily wash his hands before, then no doubt some 'qualities' WERE so imparted! The resulting dirty water was given to the patient to drink, and such was the faith in India in those days that often a cure was effected.

It is also understood that diamonds are very effective in obtaining the favours of the lady of one's desire, particularly if the diamond is wrapped up in a mink coat. But this, of course, is merely hearsay.

EMERALD: The green emerald has a reputation of being able to cure eye afflictions, and throughout the course of time people came to believe absolutely in the power of the emerald to overcome illnesses of the eye. It occurred to some warlock, or witch, or priest (they are all much the same) that if the emerald could cure eye illnesses, then it could also ward off the evil eye. And so it came to pass that emeralds were worn around the neck with the idea that if a person possessed of the evil eye looked at such a wearer all evil influences would be warded off and reflected back to the evil eye with singularly disastrous results to the latter.

There is much evidence in the East that emeralds actually did help in the alleviation of eye complaints.

GARNET: This is a stone which apparently now is not very popular, but at one time it was worn with the hope of protecting the wearer from skin diseases and danger. It had to be worn actually in contact with the body, and instead of being used in rings as at present, it was put in a little mounting and worn around the neck, usually arranged so that it was right over the heart.

When danger of ill health was present, a stone acclimatised to its wearer would become dull and lustreless. As the danger or illness abated the stone would return to its original brilliance.

At present in Europe people wear garnets in the belief that it gives them constancy in love.

JADE: Many people think of jade as a green stone, but one can have jade of quite a number of different shades. It can be almost clear, for example, or yellow, or varying shades of green, blue, or even black. Jade is a stone which can be carved and worked by those who have such skill. The Chinese, before Communism, worked jade into very beautiful ornaments and statues.

The Chinese businessman of pre-Communist days used to have his hands inside his sleeves. If you remember, they had very large sleeves, and often an astute businessman would keep his hands inside his sleeves and would clasp a talisman made of jade. He would ask the jade to guide him in a profitable business deal.

In the medical sense it is stated that a green jade could, by its particular vibration, cure dropsy and similar afflictions relating to the urinary system.

JET: Jet is a black stone. Its correct name is gaggitis. It is a stone which was of particular importance in the time of the Druids in the British Isles. A jet knife was used for the druidic sacrifices at Stonehenge.

In Ireland even at the present time, particularly on the West coast where the wild Atlantic beats against the great rocks, the Irish fisherman's wife will burn a small piece of jet stone while praying for his safe return from the perils of the turbulent sea.

Before the days of dentists people used powdered jet put around an aching tooth. Probably the sharpness of the powder gave them something else to think about, but apparently it worked in curing toothache. It also cured headache and stomach ache.

LAPIS LAZULI: This is a stone of particular history in Egypt and in India. Many plaques were inscribed on lapis lazuli cylinders, giving high esoteric knowledge. Lapis lazuli was known as one of the sacred stones, one of the stones used in the performance of the Higher Mysteries. It was sacred because of its beauty, but in the medical sense it was stated to avert miscarriage and abortions.

ONYX: In the East this is regarded as a stone of misfortune. It is an invitation to those possessed of the evil eye, and apparently it used to be quite good practice to disguise a stone of this type and make it resemble something else, or embed it in something else, and then give it to one's enemy with the conviction that the poor wretch would get more than he expected.

OPAL: This is another stone which is very unfortunate. The smoky stone mined largely in Australia often had bad influences and the occultist could detect malignant radiations.

Some people claim that opals are extremely good for those suffering from eye diseases, but if one is fortunate enough to obtain a black opal which still is light enough so that one may see the ruby 'flares' in it, then that may be considered to be a bringer of good fortune, and to give one remarkably keen sight.

RUBY: This stone is stated to protect one from all manner of infectious diseases. It is stated that rubies prevent one from having typhoid, bubonic, and other plagues.

As in the case of diamonds, the better type of ruby was often swished around in water, or even left in water for a time, and then the patient was given the water to drink when suffering from intestinal pains.

It has been known also for a person suffering from cancer of the intestines to swallow a ruby which was, 'in the course of nature,' recovered, cleaned, and swallowed again, and it is stated quite definitely that a case is known where cancer was arrested by this means.

SAPPHIRE: Many people confuse sapphires, the turquoise, and lapis lazuli, but whichever name you give it, the remarks referred to under lapis lazuli will apply in the case of the sapphire and the turquoise.

TOUCH STONES: Stones, as we have seen, are, like all other substances, merely a mass of molecules in motion. The sensation which can be imparted to a person may be for good or for evil. There are stones which radiate misfortune and cause grave disharmony within the body. But there are also stones which make one become tranquil, and these are called Tranquilliser Touch Stones.

Centuries and centuries ago, long before the age of aspirins, the Ancients, the Adepts, and the Magic Makers of old could cure humanity of their various nervous and mental ills. They could bring tranquillity into the homes of people.

In far off China, in Tibet, in the holy temples of India, and in the great temples of the Incas, the Aztecs, and the Mayas, priests laboriously shaped stones by hand, stones whose cunningly contrived contours comforted the human brain, and by flooding that organ with comfort and pleasant tactile sensations calmed the whole of the human mechanism. Unfortunately, the art of making such contoured-stones became almost extinct throughout the ages. People stuffed themselves with drugs to depress sensation, because we are in a negative cycle of evolution, and drugs make one 'negative.'

Tranquilliser Touch Stones are available once again; I have made such stones, and I have copyrighted the design because only one particular configuration offers the maximum comfort.

A Tranquilliser Touch Stone should be held in either the left or the right hand, it does not matter which. The part with my name should be against the palm, and the ideograph should be at the bottom, leaving the carefully dished portion facing upwards so that it comes under the ball of your thumb. Then your thumb should idly follow the contours in that dished portion. You will find that comfort, ease, and freedom from worry will steal upon you, you will find that your problems will dissolve away like morning mist before the rising sun. You will find that you have such peace of mind as you have not had before.

This is not the place to give further details, but you may have seen my advertisements by now. It will suffice to say that if we use the things of nature as intended, then the things of nature can come to our aid. Stones can help us quite as much as fruits and herbal remedies. It should be stated that only a suitably contoured Touch Stone should be used because the wrong sort can cause irritation instead of tranquillity. So—you have been warned!

TURQUOISE: The turquoise is very common in Tibet, where there is a bridge called 'The Turquoise Bridge.' Prayer Wheels and Charm Boxes in Tibet were usually decorated with small turquoise stones because the turquoise was known as a particularly fortunate stone.

It was mounted in rings, and worn in the hair. The Tibetan woman used to wear a large framework so that her hair could be displayed to the maximum advantage, and often the frame itself would be decorated with turquoise stones.

Turquoise stones are extremely good for giving one improved health.

The turquoise is a stone sacred in the Buddhist belief.

THE STUFF WE EAT!

As anyone who has lived on this Earth for even a little while will have discovered, we have to eat in order to live, but we should not live merely in order to eat. The human body can be likened to a factory; materials are taken in and 'worked' and changed in various ways. In our human factory materials are taken in so that the body may maintain itself, repair tissue which has been damaged or aged, and to drive the muscles which move one about. There also must be enough materials left over so that the body can grow mentally and physically.

Humans need four basic types of material in order that tissue may grow or be repaired, and in order that bones may grow or re-unite after fracture. Here alphabetically are the four things quite essential to human life:

1. Carbohydrates.
2. Hydrocarbons.
3. Minerals.
4. Protein.

Before Man became civilised—or considered himself civilised—all mankind was vegetarian, but in those days the appendix, that now troublesome or atrophied organ, had a very useful part in the life of the human body, and as the appendix is just an atrophied stump, then Man should not be entirely vegetarian. To be a vegetarian and to be in any way the equivalent of a balanced eater means that one must be eating all the time, because one has to take in vast bulk of a purely vegetarian diet.

Mankind became acclimatised to meat, and found that by eating reasonable amounts of meat one could manage with less fruit and vegetables, and so there was more time away from eating to devote to other things.

Many people are too 'bitter.' That is, their blood, juices, and tissues contain too much acid, and such people crave bitter or sharp things such as lemons, sour apples, and all manner of things which have a sharp, tangy, acid taste. This is unfortunate because such people get too much acid in the blood and that depletes the blood's capacity for taking carbon dioxide and other waste gases which have to be exhaled. It requires an alkaline blood to absorb gases which have to be carried to the lungs and exhaled, thus making room for oxygen to be inhaled.

So—all you who like bitter things, remember that you are upsetting your oxygenation system! In addition, you lay yourself wide open for colds, chest complaints, rheumatism, and nerve upsets.

It is unfortunate that vegetarians often become cranks and faddists; they become extreme! It has already been stated that a vegetarian diet is an ideal diet FOR THOSE WHO LIVE IN IDEAL CONDITIONS. If one is a vegetarian, and living in the ideal conditions which that demands, there is no such complaint as constipation, because the bulk of waste and rough cellulose with its hydrogogic properties lubricates the large intestine, and aids in the expelling of waste products. But again, in order to live as a purely vegetarian person one has to be more or less eating all the time.

Constipation is most frequently caused because the blood extracts too much moisture from the intestines. By the time the waste products have reached the descending colon there is not enough moisture in it to make it pliable (or 'plastic') so that it can be expelled. Such waste matter then adheres quite firmly to the hairlike lining of the colon, and muscular contractions called peristalsis causes pain. People would be less costive if they drank more water.

VITAMINS: Vitamins are 'life forces.' They are present in the four essential materials which we mentioned before; vitamins are present in fruit, vegetables, and nuts, and in most of the natural substances which we eat. These 'life essences' are a definite requirement, and if one lacks certain of them one is subject to all manner of unpleasant illnesses. Lack of vitamins, for instance, is the cause of beri-beri, and in Japanese prisoner-of-war camps beri-beri could often be cured when the patient could get hold of a little Marmite, a most valuable product.

In the days of the old sailing-ships, before refrigeration and all that, when the 'wooden walls of England' sailed the seas, without having to wonder about the Russian fishing fleets, sailors often suffered from scurvy. This is a skin disease caused by lack of vitamins, and if scurvy is neglected eventually the sufferer 'fades away,' becomes worse and worse in health, and eventually dies. It starts as a skin disease, and then works its way inwards and affects various organs.

In the days of those sailing-ships English sailors took lime juice aboard because lime juice was rich in vitamins, and this lime juice was issued in much the same way as rum was issued. That lime juice, by the way, is why Americans call English people 'limeys,' because of the lime juice, or lime fruit, consumed aboard British ships.

Unless one has adequate vitamins one is not able to break down or to assimilate the minerals which also are necessary to us. A correct mixture of vitamins and minerals must be maintained, otherwise our various glands, such as endocrines, will not function correctly, then people lack hormones, testrone, they become sterile—impotent. They become irritable and become victims to all manner of obscure complaints. Here are some of the essential vitamins:

VITAMIN 'A': We depend greatly upon vitamin A, which is a substance soluble in fats and oils. It helps to keep the skin in a suitable pliable and unbroken condition. It helps to prevent infection through abrasions of the skin, and it is a most useful aid in overcoming urinary illnesses. A further advantage is that a sufficient quantity of vitamin A is of great benefit in regulating oxygenation of the brain.

VITAMIN 'B1': Vitamin B1 is not soluble by acids, but is

destroyed completely by an excessively alkaline condition. Thus, unless we maintain our body juices or secretions at the optimum level between excess acidity and excess alkalinity, we are going to destroy many substances before they can help us at all. Vitamin B1 gives one a good appetite and aids the digestion of that which it has induced us to eat. It helps provide adequate resistance to infection, and is one of the essential materials if we are to have proper growth.

VITAMIN 'B2': Vitamin B2 is a water-soluble vitamin. It is a substance particularly essential for good vision. If one lacks this vitamin one is always having eyesight trouble, and many such ailments can be overcome by attention to the vitamin content of the body.

This vitamin assists in the smooth functioning of the alimentary canal from start to finish. It provides one with good digestive powers, and enables one to 'eat like a horse!'

If one lacks vitamin B2, the system cannot absorb iron, and further a lack of this vitamin causes severe loss of hair, and so depletes the resources of the body that one suffers from ulcers such as ulcers of the tongue, etc.

VITAMIN 'C': Vitamin C is an unstable substance. It cannot be stored very long in the body. Any imbalance will cause attacks on this vitamin, and cause it to be destroyed before it can be properly utilised. One needs to take this substance every day, and one's diet should be so arranged so that there is an adequate supply.

Vitamin C is beneficial for bone and tooth growth because it makes it possible for the body to absorb calcium, which, as you know, is a requirement for sound quality bones. Without vitamin C the body becomes rickety through lack of calcium. Lack of the vitamin causes respiratory troubles, and may make one prone to T.B.

VITAMIN 'D': Vitamin D is another of the vitamins which regulates the calcium and phosphorous absorption, and enables phosphorous to become phosphates. So unless we have vitamin D we are not able to make the best use of the minerals which we also must have that our body functions may continue.

Vitamin D is one of the things which the vegetarian usually lacks, because this is NOT found in vegetable or fruits. The faddist vegetarian must get his vitamin D from artificial sources instead of going to natural meat.

Too much vitamin D will give you severe illness such as

acute depression, and diarrhoea; you will be unable then to retain food long enough for the villi—the hairlike tubes in the intestines—to absorb the food, so in effect you will suffer from starvation in the midst of plenty.

VITAMIN 'E': Vitamin E (we can go through the alphabet with these letters!) is a substance which lodges in the muscles and, unfortunately, rapidly becomes destroyed or excreted. Thus it is that we must have a balanced diet in order to ensure a regular supply of vitamin E. Lack of this produces sterility and miscarriages, and when a child is born it is handicapped from then on.

For those who are interested, celery and germ of wheat are the most suitable sources of Vitamin E.

Now we have dealt with our vitamins perhaps we should give a note about the minerals which are necessary to us.

MINERALS: Minerals are quite essential, and the confirmed vegetarian should remember that many minerals are present in meat as well as in fruit and vegetables. Thus, a balanced diet of meat and vegetables and fruit gives a more balanced supply of vitamins and minerals.

In the ideal world people would not eat meat, but we do not live in such idyllic conditions. We have to get up in the morning before we are really ready to eat, then we have to rush through breakfast, rush to catch a bus, at the office we have to work in a cramped and unnatural position. At lunch-time we have to rush out to get some food to keep us going, and at the same time as we are hurrying through our food we are talking to other people. We hasten back to the office, get cramped again, and after that we might do a long journey home too tired, too dispirited, too frustrated, to be in a suitable state to really digest the food which is placed before us. A real vegetarian meal should be a rather leisurely affair lasting most of the day, and it cannot sensibly be accomplished under everyday living conditions. So—for those who are cranky about vegetarianism, they can only be logical if they go to some far-off isle away from the snares, delusions, and illusions of civilisation. If they want to stay here, then they are advised to take the path of sweet reasonableness, and eat enough meat to maintain the essential functions of the body.

Here are the essential minerals arranged alphabetically:

CALCIUM: Calcium is quite necessary if one is to have strong bones and sound teeth. Calcium is the foundation of our bones and our teeth. Without calcium one would soon bleed to death even after a slight scratch, because this mineral gives the blood clotting ability.

Calcium aids in the absorption of vitamin D, and these two work together.

CHLORINE: Everyone knows that chlorine is a good cleaner. You can buy bottles of the stuff under various trade names and use it for doing your dishes or your washing. In the human body chlorine is necessary, in limited quantities, of course, for the chlorine which we take cleans and disinfects the body cells, purifies the blood, helps in ridding the body of excessive accumulations of unwanted fats, and eliminates various impurities which get in one's joints and make one creak like a rusty hinge when one moves.

Chlorine in controlled amounts is essential, and if one has a balanced diet one finds that there are adequate supplies of chlorine in the everyday meals which we have.

COPPER: Copper is necessary, as we wrote before, in order that, together with chlorophyll (the latter coming from all green stuff of course), iron may be broken down to a form that the body can take and use. We shall deal with iron later.

Copper can be classed as one of the 'trace elements' because even a minute amount is enough to act as a catalyst. A catalyst is that which can act on another substance without necessarily becoming changed or destroyed in the process.

Science has not discovered precisely how much copper is necessary, but even a minute trace will be adequate, and the ordinary balanced diet contains the necessary amount.

IODINE: Iodine is quite essential for the correct functioning of the body. Everyone knows that seaweed (kelp) is rich in iodine, and another suitable source is sea food.

Some time ago people used to wear lockets containing a dab of iodine, but this was a mere psychological affair because the iodine has to be absorbed, and normal food contains adequate supplies.

Iodine can cure goitre because that complaint is merely a disfunction of the thyroid gland. Iodine corrects a deficiency and helps to regulate that gland. In many places remote from the sea the natives of the place suffer from goitre, but it is rare indeed for a person to have goitre when living by the side of the sea, because even the rain contains a certain amount of iodine unless one is in a far distant area.

IRON: Iron is another mineral. People who think of it as a metal forget that it is still a mineral. Probably everyone knows that we need iron, because without it we are not able to manufacture the red blood corpuscles which enables our blood stream to absorb oxygen. If we lack oxygen our brain becomes dull and eventually dies. So iron is a very, very necessary mineral.

We cannot swallow a few nuts and bolts and say that we have had some iron. The iron has to be in a certain form and then it has to be acted upon by chlorophyll and copper in order that it can undergo a chemical change within the body so that the various body cells can absorb it and use it.

It is interesting to note that the ladies require more than their share of iron; the ladies need about four times as much iron for the same body-weight as a man. This is because the former have various outputs which a man is delighted to avoid.

MAGNESIUM: Magnesium is a mineral which assists calcium in forming bones. If we lack magnesium we are prone to tooth decay. It is quite an essential as is calcium.

Magnesium helps in the digestive system, in fact if one gets a pain through indigestion (probably through eating too much!) you cure the complaint by taking some magnesium tablets.

We need an alkaline form of magnesium, and that can conveniently be obtained from nuts and in most types of fruit.

PHOSPHOROUS: We also have to have phosphorous, you know, stuff which makes the ordinary kitchen match strike. Phosphorous is a highly combustible material. You may have seen experiments in a laboratory where a piece of phosphorous was taken out of the water in which it is usually stored. Immediately it is so removed, and in the presence of air with its oxygen, it starts to smoulder and give off dense white smoke.

Phosphorous helps greatly in oxidising various substances in the body and in giving alkalinity to the blood.

Without having this alkaline blood we cannot get rid of excess gases such as carbon dioxide. If we have our blood stream cluttered up with carbon dioxide and excess nitrogen, then we have a 'cyanosed' or blue appearance, because our blood is then oxygen starved. Phosphorous overcomes this by making room for oxygen.

Phosphorous compounds are necessary in order to maintain

the health of our nervous system. Phosphorous when used for nerves is termed 'lecithins.' This strengthens the white stuff of the nervous system and the nervous tissue which is found in the grey matter of the brain. Thus, if we lack phosphorous we also lack brain power. Fish is a food rich in phosphorous and phosphates, that is why people say that fish is good food for the brain.

POTASSIUM: Potassium is a mineral which ensures that our muscles remain elastic. If one were without potassium the intercostal and heart muscles would fail, and so this mineral is absolutely essential to the maintenance of life. Fortunately, the alkaline type which we need is present in most species of fruits and vegetables, and thus should cause no difficulty in acquiring a suitable supply.

SODIUM: Sodium of the alkaline variety is of benefit to human beings in addition to being of use in street lamps of the fluorescent type. Sodium is one of our most important products at the present time.

Deficiency of sodium can actually cause diabetes, because its lack may be the instigator of paralysis of the Islets of the pancreas. When these Islets are paralysed the person is not able to break down the sugars and fats. Many people who suffer from diabetes would be helped by taking alkaline sodium in their diet.

How to obtain alkaline sodium? Eat bananas, celery, lettuce, and a very prolific source of many minerals are chestnuts—preferably lightly boiled and roasted.

If a person lacks sodium he will also lack saliva, and there will be a paucity of bile and pancreatic juices.

SULPHUR: Sulphur is a mineral known to the witches of old. A dose of sulphur and brimstone used to work wonders for people in love! Sulphur is a very good blood tonic and conditioner. It was also given to animals so that their fur should be preserved, and for the same reason sometimes a lady will dust sulphur powder into the fur coat which she has laboriously obtained.

The acid type of sulphur is essential for all cells of the body. It is an antiseptic of the blood cells, and it helps purify the cells around the intestines.

Without an adequate supply of acid sulphur one can be the victim of a weird and unpleasant collection of skin diseases. Sulphur also helps to make hair grow.

This is not meant to be a learned treatise on diet, but should be read as notes intended to help you work out your own food problems. Throughout *all* my books I say what I feel, what I consider to be fact. Possibly some people might think that 'fools rush in where angels fear to tread,' but I know what I am doing (which most people do not!), and I want to say this:

Man is an animal. Man has certain animal requirements. At present, because we have broken away from nature, and live in a 'civilised' world where there are all manner of unnecessary jobs, we have to eat synthetic foods, messed up foods, stuff which has been put through processes which kill off many of the most important constituents; vitamins have been rendered insoluble, and a lot of minerals have been 'filtered' out.

So let us be sensible; at our present stage of evolution we may have to eat a certain amount of meat, but we can still have our vegetables, our fruits, and our nuts. Let us not ruin our health by denying ourselves meat IF THE BODY NEEDS IT. Some people do not need it, for others it is essential. You can only 'let your conscience be your guide.'

Many people think that it is cruel to eat meat. According to Russian scientists who have used special equipment of an electronic nature, and have inserted probes into poor suffering plants, a cabbage can shriek with pain when it is cut. Scientists throughout the world have been doing researches into the reflexes and responses of fruits and vegetables, and it has been found that these do have sense-reflexes which react to certain stimuli.

If you are going to be logical, if you are so cranky that you will not eat meat, then why eat butter? Why drink milk? Think of this; to supply the milk which you are willing to drink some poor wretched cow has had violent hands laid upon a rather sensitive portion of her anatomy. That portion has been rudely manipulated in order to separate the cow from the milk—in order to give you some pleasure.

If you kill an animal for meat it is done cleanly and in-stantaneously. But if you are going to take the view that this is unkind, well, why put a cow through the torture of being milked twice a day?

And if you still insist that you will not destroy any life in order to eat, how about all the germs, all the bacteria, on a lettuce when you chew it? And how are you going to satisfy your conscience when you look at the lettuce leaf you have been chewing and find half a worm?

Let us be sensible, let us eat that which is necessary to us at our present stage or level of development. We can always hope that with our continued evolution we shall be able to dispense with meat, synthetic foods, water with fluorides in it, air which has been contaminated, etc., and go back to nature, fig leaves, and woad. Then only shall we be ready to live on a purely vegetable and fruit diet. Otherwise if we become cranks, then we do not merely chew nuts, we *are* 'nuts!'

SUPPLEMENT D

EXERCISES

THERE is no doubt whatever that exercises and disciplines are a very popular feature of the writings of many authors. For that reason I thought that I should add a few notes stating why I am so definitely opposed to irresponsible exercises.

Many, if not all, of the Yogic exercises originated in the Far East where people are taught and practise such things from babyhood up to the time of their death. These Yogic exercises form quite an important part of what one might call the lower-class Easterner's life.

The higher-trained Adept does not use Yogic exercises, they are not necessary for such people. The purpose of Yogic exercises is to discipline the human body. When a person reaches the state when he can discipline his mind, then he has progressed far beyond the stage at which he needs to tie his legs around his neck while balancing on one thumb, or something like it.

In my considered opinion, based on many years of observation, it is dangerous for the average middle-aged Western man or woman to suddenly, enthusiastically take up exercises which are suitable only for very supple-boned people, or those who have been trained from the very earliest days.

For a person suffering from hardened arteries, or various other conditions, to take up exercises is both foolish and hazardous, and can lead to grave risk of impairing the health.

Throughout my writings I have stressed the dangers of unsupervised exercises for the Westerner. If you want to do some exercises do that suggested under 'Neck,' or a few simple and mild things, and practise the breathing exercises in Supplement A.

It is necessary for the unevolved occultist to master his or her body before being able to master his or her mind, in the same way that children may play with tops or hoops. But for those who have progressed beyond such elementary things Yogic exercises are a waste of time.

In India and similar countries the contortionist tying himself in knots, or who has held an arm above his head until it has atrophied, is not an Adept, he is just a contortionist, a street performer, one who has little spirituality perhaps, one who has to make his living by doing these stage turns in much the same way as one can see buskers on the streets of big cities and outside theatres.

The real Adept does not give demonstrations, and, in fact, the real Adept does not go in for these exercises.

I have tried to warn you, so if you go in for the plough position, or some of these other things, and you get a crick in your back that is your own fault. If, in disregarding this warning, you start to raise the Kundalini and then cannot control it, well—you started it.

My strong recommendation is that if you are more than eighteen or twenty years of age you should not indulge in any strenuous exercises or contortions unless you are thoroughly accustomed to these things, because it is painfully easy (and painful to suffer!) to strain muscles, displace bones, and generally upset your health. So—if you are wise leave these exercises unless you have some really genuine Eastern-trained occultist who can help you and supervise you, and keep you from harm.

Occultism, as well as religion, can be a joyous thing if we will permit it to be so. But if we unnecessarily complicate it with all sorts of really stupid things, then we have only ourselves to blame for miseries which will surely come.

The exercises given in this book, in fact, any exercise which I give, is safe and healthy, except when I tell you with a note of considerable derision that you should not attempt it, where I tell you, in fact, to show you what others go in for!

I hope that you enjoyed this book, and that it will bring you a lot of help, satisfaction, and health.

A SELECTED LIST OF PSYCHIC, MYSTIC AND OCCULT TITLES FROM CORGI